Through Their Eyes: The Quill Took Flight

THROUGH THEIR EYES: THE QUILL TOOK FLIGHT

An Anthology of Student Writings

Editors
Dr. Patricia H. Graham
Ms. Amy Russ
Ms. Kay Wolf

E-BookTime, LLC
Montgomery, Alabama

Through Their Eyes: The Quill Took Flight
An Anthology of Student Writings

Edited by Dr. Patricia H. Graham, Ms. Amy Russ, Ms. Kay Wolf

ISBN: 978-1-60862-704-2

First Edition
Published August 2017
E-BookTime, LLC
6598 Pumpkin Road
Montgomery, AL 36108
www.e-booktime.com

About the Cover Design

Like a phoenix rising from the fire, so are our students at Southwestern Community College. In Greek folklore, the phoenix is given a second chance to relive and gain new experiences for growth. The phoenix is seen rising from the ashes, discarding the old ways, and taking flight into a new direction. Within this depiction, there are varieties of colors portrayed in this bird. This is significant because within a community college, we too have many diverse cultures enrolled in the *Educational Opportunities Program*. We believe as educators that all students are welcome and deserve as many chances as possible for improving their way of life. We would like to see all of our students fulfill the potential of becoming a new, vibrant phoenix by challenging all expectations placed upon them, whether this be in society, economically, or academically.

We hope you enjoy this book as much as the students did writing their short works.

Foreword

Through Their Eyes: The Quill Took Flight is an anthology of short works written by students enrolled in the Educational Opportunities Program of Southwestern Community College, in Sylva, North Carolina. A grant was made possible by Southwestern Foundation's Grant Committee for these students to publish their writings who otherwise would have never been published. These works were compiled to demonstrate the writing abilities of second language learners, who are learning English, and American adult learners, who are working on their high-school equivalency.

Within this book, readers will find poetry, fiction, and non-fiction depicting the students' native language and English writing abilities. Additionally, readers will have a front row seat, to visualize, through the students' eyes, their culture, dreams, and life. Cultures represented in these stories include: Gujarati, Chinese, Vietnamese, Spanish, Arabic, Thai, and English (formal and Appalachian). Although the readers may not comprehend the orthography of these second language learners, it is important to see the struggles and transitions from interchangeably moving from one language to another. The majority of the second language learners have only been in the United States a few months. Therefore, the depth of the sentence structures is not quite fully developed. However, the basic sentence structures are in place.

Arabic To English

ترادتيون العربية للنساء

مرحبا..
أسمي جميلة وأنا من السعودية. من أهم عادات وتقاليد اجدادنا وأمهاتنا السعوديات تعلم أطفالها على بر وطاعة الوالدين وخدمتهم والإعتناء فيهم وتلبية طلباتهم من الصغر الى الكبر ، عشان اذا كبروا يبرون عيالهم فيهم ويخدمونهم مثل ماكانوا والدينهم يخدمونهم لما كانوا أطفال،
وتوارثت هذه العاده عندنا من جيل الى جيل اخر
ولايمكن أن تكون التربيه بغير هذه العاده

Wehmid-Al, Jameelah
© 2017
Saudi

The Arabic Tradition of Women

My name, Jameelah, means beautiful in Arabic, and I am from Saudi Arabia. One of the most important customs and traditions of our grandparents, the elders before them, and Saudi mothers today is the teaching of being respectful. Saudi mothers are expected to teach their children about righteousness, obedience to parents, and give their love and care for children while meeting their demands from childhood to adulthood. When the children grow up, their children will be respected and served, as well as their children. This tradition has been passed on to us from generation to generation. Educating our children cannot be without this standard.

Jameelah Al-Wehimid
© 2017
Saudi

Chinese To English

中国春节

春节是中国最重要的节日。春节是庆祝日历上的农历新年。在春节到来的前一天晚上，家家户户要团聚在一起吃丰盛的大餐。 每年都会庆祝一只动物。今年是2017年，是公鸡的一年。公鸡是雄性和力量的象征。在很多地方的人们还喜欢燃放鞭炮。过年的最传统的主食莫过于水饺了。这是孩子们非常喜欢的节日，因为他们可以吃美食，穿新衣。当然他们还可以拿到他们父母亲戚给的压岁钱。拿到钱的小朋友会交到好的运气。人们会把春联贴在墙上象征吉祥如意。 春节会持续15天之久，人们在拜访亲朋好友时会说：“（过年好）万事如意。”之类的话语。人们很喜欢过春节，因为在过春节这期间他们可以好好的休息一下。

Ming Cheng

Chinese

Chinese New Year

The Spring Festival is the most important festival in China. It is a celebration of the lunar calendar's new year. Each year, an animal is celebrated. This year is 2017, and it is the Year of the Rooster. The rooster is symbolic for virility and strength.

In the evening before the Spring Festival, families get together and have a big meal. In many places, people like to set off fire-crackers. Dumplings are the most traditional food. Children like the festival very much because they can have delicious food and wear new clothes. They can also get some money from their parents. This money is given to children for good luck.

People put New Year scrolls on the wall for good fortune. The Spring Festival lasts about fifteen days long. People visit relatives and friends with the words, "May all of your wishes come true." People enjoy the Spring Festival during this time so they can have a good rest.

Ming Cheng
© 2017
Chinese

English

The Legend of Spearfinger

My Cherokee Legend

Hello, my name is Taylor, and I am a member of the Eastern Band of Cherokee Indians. When growing up as a child on the Indian reservation, I was always reminded that I must be a good boy or Spearfinger would come and steal me away during the night. Spearfinger is the Cherokee Indian's version of the boogieman. It was often said that my people would hear her screams echoing from the Great Smoky Mountains, and these screams would sound like a cackling old witch. Spearfinger, or as my people would call her, "Utlunta," was a shapeshifter.

The story goes that Utlunta could shift into one of the most respected elders of the tribe or shift into something as simple as an old woman in the village. Spearfinger was well-known to eat the liver or kidneys of children that she had poisoned. She would trick the children to helping her, and when they did not know it, she would poke the children's side with her stony finger thus making them sick. Her flesh was also made of stone. No weapon known to man could kill this horrible monster.

As more and more children grew sick in the village, the elders became concerned that their children would die from this old hag and her evil ways. Spearfinger was very sneaky and she would disguise herself as smoke or fog hidden among the brushfires and bonfires during the fall season. This made it very hard for the tribal members to search for her and kill her. One day Utlunta even disguised herself as a child so she could walk among the village people waiting to snatch her next victim. However, the village was alerted by a member of tribe, and the parents hid their children within their huts. This made Utlunta very angry. She threw big rocks down in the valley creating bridges so she could travel faster from one village to another. The tribal elders decided they had to stop Utlunta.

The medicine man told his people, "We need to dig a very deep pit and camouflage it with leaves and twigs. We will hunt Spearfinger and chase her toward the direction of the pit. When she falls in, she will be trapped there forever." When the trap was finished, the hunters built a bonfire, hoping to lure Utlunta to them. When Utlunta appeared to them, one young brave said, "She is not Spearfinger but just an old woman." But, the medicine man was much wiser than this brave and he threw a spear at this old woman. The spear bounced off of this old lady's chest, and then the braves knew this was Spearfinger in disguise. This made the Utlunta very angry and she began to chase the young men.

The young braves knew she would chase them, and they began running toward the pit. Spearfinger did not see the pit, and she fell deep into the hole. The young braves tried to pierce her chest with their spears but they just bounced off of her. This angered Spearfinger even more. She gathered all of the spears in the pit and cursed horrible profanities to the young Indians, and she began to climb out of the pit.

The young men grew very scared of Utlunta. "Oh what shall we do? How shall we kill this horrible monster?" cried the braves. A blue jay flew down and spoke to the brave warriors and began to sing a song, "♫un, un, un, un ♫." The braves thought the blue jay was telling them to aim for Utlunta's heart. They all aimed for her heart, and once again the spears bounced off of her. The young braves had now become very angry with the blue jay, and they tried to kill him. But the blue jay flew away, never to be seen again. Then a hummingbird flew toward the hag and landed on her palm, and it began to sing. The young warriors again threw their spears at Spearfinger and pierced her hand. This was her undoing because her heart was hidden in her hand and was the source of her power. Spearfinger let out a shrill yell and she began to fall to the ground. The Cherokee remember the hummingbird and it is honored in North Carolina. The Cherokee called the Hummingbird "Walela." This means one who intercedes on behalf of the people. The cries of

Spearfinger was heard high in the mountain tops by another creature, Stoneskin. Stoneskin knew he had been warned. If you see a hummingbird today in Cherokee, it is a reminder to Stoneskin to stay away from the Great Smoky Mountains because he will protect the people as he did many years ago.

Lewis Taylor Niccum
© 2017
Cherokee Indian

I Am Your Brother

You would think growing up on an Indian reservation would be an adventure for a young boy. But on the contrary, life proved to be quite challenging. The young Indian boys would use to call me "Uneg" shortened for *white boy* in the Cherokee language. Life for a half-breed was extremely difficult living in two worlds where nobody would claim you as part of their race.

My father raised me as a Cherokee brave. I was taught to be proud of my heritage even though I lived in two existing worlds. I would often retreat to the woods to play, and later in life to reflect what it meant to be half white and half Cherokee male. The woods became my solace, my refuge, and my playground. Here, I could retreat from all of the prejudices and labels I faced daily in my life.

Living as a Cherokee brave and as a white child proved to be difficult in its own standards, but I had also endured many health issues too. I had to have surgery as a young child on my own and received a pacemaker and an artificial heart valve. I was limited in my abilities to endure the physical activities as a child, which my companions had taken for granted. Early in life, I was given the title of being "special." I began to believe I had no worth.

"Special" back then carried a negative connotation. However, as I grew older, I discovered I had a passion for clay. It was through my hands, I learned that I could connect my Cherokee heritage and my "whiteness" through pottery. All of the labels and prejudices that I had faced disappear when my hands begin to mold my creations. My mind is always clear. I have an image in my mind's eye and eventually, a work of art is created. The clay becomes alive and a piece of me is carried on to another who purchases my pottery.

Today the word "special" has taken on a new meaning in my life. I am in a unique position to live in two worlds, and I can coexist and benefit from both. I am constantly proving that worlds can be balanced. I have found my own path and the *Great Father* is always beside me on my life's journey. Now, I am known as *Ayeli iyv dinadantli*, half-brother of the Eastern Band of the Cherokee Indian Nation.

Lewis Taylor Niccum
© 2017
Cherokee Indian

Vacation

My favorite vacation was Walt Disney world. I was eight years old the first time we went. We lived in Sylva, North Carolina and drove fifteen hours to get there. The car was loaded up with my mom, dad, sister, and me. We looked like we were a school bus full of crazy kids, and all the pillows in the back seat of the Pontiac Grand Am were like marshmallows. I was so happy we were on our way. We left out at 5 a.m. for Florida. Disney, the Magic Kingdom where dreams are made, was waiting on me with all it had to offer. The excitement was building.

When we got to the Magic Kingdom, it was 7 p.m. It was dark and hot, but my mom and dad said we could eat there and see the electrical parade. The lights were everywhere and so magical. The slushy cups had lights in them and were so vibrant. We did get to go on rides in the dark, and had a different feel to it. At night the rides felt like they were going faster than they do in the day. It was like magic to see it at night and get to go back in the day. It was two different atmospheres. I remember my mom and dad fighting about money. My mom wanted my sister and I to have the whole shebang, but my dad wanted us to have fun too but with a budget. My mom and dad had fun too even though they would not admit it.

When I was a child, Disney was so fun with the sun on my skin and the smell of cotton candy in the air and the smell of the sea water in the air. The landscape was enchanting as if it was in the medieval days, and there's water everywhere even a moat around the castle surrounded by wisteria, pampas grass. It's so cartoonish.

They have a lot of characters, some of my favorite are Mickey Mouse, Snow White, Peter Pan, Maleficent. Some new ones we had never heard of. They scared the hell out of me so I cried when they would get close to us. But not my big sister, she was not scared of them I remember thinking how cool my sister was. So we have pictures of her with them but not me. I could have been one of the characters because of my bowl hair cut my mom gave me. All I would have need was wooden shoes. I could have been a character from It's a Small World.

The rides were great. We rode the teacups, and my dad got so dizzy that he could not walk straight. My sister rode the Dumbo ride with me. I loved it because you could hit a button and make it go up and down. Mom rode It's a Small World with me because it had air conditioning. We loved it because it was eighty-five degrees that day.

Disney is the most magical place in the world because it is enchanting and it brings my family together. I will always have the memories of us at Disney. The electrical parade, getting to see the Magic Kingdom, the landscape, the smell of cotton candy, Mickey Mouse, and rides. It was so sunny and warm and nice. My mom did whatever it took to make it magical for my sis and me. We had a great childhood growing up, and my parents still to this day work hard to make things happen for us, my sister, grand kids, and me.

Michael Middleton
© 2017
American

Carolina Ginseng (Sang)

Hi, my name is Charles, and I am going to discuss the heritage and preservation of North Carolina ginseng. There are many different varieties of ginseng in the United States. The preservation and conservation of ginseng needs to be maintained in North Carolina or future generations will lose a significant part of their heritage. I am a mountain man who raises, harvests, and sells Carolina ginseng. There are a variety of uses as well as laws, to understanding why ginseng is an essential part of North Carolina's heritage.

As a child in the Great Smoky Mountains, my family and I spent a lot of time in the mountains. Fishing, hunting, and harvesting ginseng is a way of life. The ways of the old are slowly leaving. As times changes, we are forced to change with it. Walking the mountains, seeing, and understanding the conservation and preservation of this plant is crucial to our heritage. Teaching our children to be able to live off the land, to garden, to hunt mushrooms, berries and find ginseng is an economical advantage for the local people.

There are many different things that can be harvested for money. Bloodroot, chestnut oak moss, and smoke vine would bring additional money into the family income. Running trap lines and selling furs as a child was fun to me. But digging ginseng was one of my passions because getting to walk in the woods and doing something that I love was an adventure. But most importantly, I understood the importance of keeping this plant from being on the endangered list, which is up to you and me. Over digging and harvesting plants that are not of age can be detrimental to future plant growth. Taking this plant before the berries are ripe has hurt this plant.

When I was a child, my father would take us to the mountains walking through briar thickets looking for this plant. My legs were constantly scratched and bloody from the briars. And no one has ever experienced picking ginseng with jiggers digging in their skin.

The preservation and conservation of this plant has taken a great transformation for the worst. More demand has made this plant hard to find. The demand for this plant has increased the price because the demand for this plant is much higher due to its medicinal purposes. The laws are constantly changing every season! People have taken the price increase as a means of employment. In the fall, the woods come alive with people in hopes of finding this elusive plant, not understanding the repercussions and the laws of harvesting ginseng.

This plant is a seed bearing plant, but it will not bear seeds every year due to the weather and the slowly changing environment. The winters have grown mild and the ground doesn't freeze. Cool temperatures make the plants come up and bear seed. The deep mountain coves and steep mountain ranges hold dark lush vegetation that sustains places for this plant to hide. Ginseng grows under Spicewood, near creeks, and the most snake infested briar thickets. This plant has become very hard to find. Ginseng has a way of trying to conceal itself.

I would like to express that ginseng is not as abundant as it used to be. Even though it was a cash crop back then, and even still today, the scarcity of the plant is making it much harder to locate and secure. This is why the conservation of this plant has become even more important. Future generations will soon only see pictures of a plant that was once indigenous to the Great Smoky Mountains. This is a beautiful plant and it can offer so much to humanity. As an Appalachian man, I think we should all protect nature and her environment so that we can all enjoy what she has to offer. If you get a chance, please be sure to travel through the Great Smoky Mountains and see what it has to offer. I know I have found a little bit of heaven here myself, and I think you would too.

Charles Brooks

American

Naughty or Nice

As a child, I always looked forward to Christmas time: opening the presents, enjoying good food, decorating the Christmas tree, and spending time with my extended family were just a few of the things I looked forward to. However, I always made sure to be on my best behavior, particularly when Christmas was approaching. But not for the reasons you would be led to believe. I wasn't afraid of being put on Santa Claus's "Naughty List" or even of getting coal in my stocking instead of presents under the tree. My reason for behaving so well around Christmas time can be summed up into one word: Krampus.

Every year on December first, my mom and dad would sit me and my siblings down in the living room after decorating the Christmas tree and tell us the story of Santa Claus and his vile sidekick, Krampus. As you may well know, Santa dresses in a red coat, pants, and hat with white fur trim and black boots. He is a very jolly person who works hard all year around in his workshop to make sure all the boys and girls get presents. Throughout the year, he keeps an eye on children all around the world and makes a list of who has been naughty and who has been nice. If you made the nice list, you would be rewarded on Christmas morning with presents under the tree. Be that as it may, if you made the naughty list you weren't so lucky.

If you made the naughty list, you would be visited by a half-demon named Krampus on the night of Christmas Eve or December 24. Krampus is born out of German folklore. He is depicted as a dark, hairy, horned goat-like monster with a forked tongue. Unfortunately, his appearance wasn't the worst part of the story. He would come into your home and spank ill-behaved children with a bundle of sticks and take them away in a wicker basket to live in his underworld lair with him for one year. If he felt that wasn't punishment enough, he would lead children off of cliffs, force kids to beg for mercy, and sadistic ear-pulling. He was even known to drown children in ink and fish out their corpses with a pitchfork if they had been especially naughty.

My parents even went as far as getting Krampus figurines to place around our house to motivate us to behave all year around. Needless to say, my siblings and I were never naughty enough to get to meet him for ourselves. So when Christmas comes around this year think of your children. Would you like them to be rewarded by jolly St. Nick? Or will you allow them to fall victim to Krampus and his evil ways?

Bethany Peralta
©2017
American

Growing Up on an Appalachian Farm

Growing up on a farm in the Appalachian Mountains with my grandparents was great. No matter what reason, there was always something to do to keep you busy. Many memories were made and stories were told along the way. I grew up an outdoors person, whether it was working or just having fun.

In the spring, just as it started to get warm, we would all start getting everything prepared and ready for the year. We would start by getting all of our horse bridles and harnesses cleaned and ready to go. We would put the harnesses on the horses and then it was plowing time. There's nothing like the smell of horses after a hard day's work. We would spend days planting the garden and all the flowers everywhere. There were always new sounds on the farm from where all the baby animals were being born. My favorite new critters were the cows and horses. Ramp digging was something we always did every year. We would pack a lunch and set off into the woods for the day just walking and digging up the ramps. Our family put them in lots of things from meatloaf to eggs or potatoes.

Then came summer. We would stay a little busier from all the weeding in the garden to keeping squirrels and rabbits out of it. After the weeding, we would go walking and collect all the fruits and berries that were getting ripe. My grandpa loved the blackberries and made cobblers all the time. Then we would go split some wood and start getting it stacked and ready to use come winter time. After a hard day's work, we would relax, unwind, and go fishing. I remember my grandpa always telling me that when we went fishing not to let my shadow hit the water or I would scare all the fish away.

Fall was my favorite time of year. We would start collecting vegetables out of the garden and either freezing it or canning it. We went hunting for extra meat for the freezer. My favorite was deer hunting, but we also went turkey hunting. A few times a year when the fog was thick, I remember going with my family to some kin folks houses and we would go through the woods to where the stills were and help make moonshine. They waited till then so that the law wouldn't see all the smoke coming off it and get caught.

The least favorite time of year for me was winter. We had to stay inside a lot. We would go out for wood to put on the fire that we kept going to stay warm. I remember my grandpa yelling through the house early in the morning when the stove would go out during the night. On the rare occasion that our water froze, we would have to go get snow and melt it on top of the stove so we could either wash dishes or flush a toilet. I remember every winter my grandma would sit for hours near the stove and just crochet away. She would sit and say she needed to get a good start on all her baby blankets since it was cold. Her excuse was that in the winter it was "baby making season" in the mountains and everyone would be having babies coming around September from where people got bored and needed to stay warm.

In conclusion, growing up in the mountains there was always something to do. Every season was different with so many different things to do, and from learning how to do things to listening to stories that had been told for generations.

Crystal Wood

American

Cherish Your Children

I always knew growing up that I wanted to be a mother. I would spend hours taking care of my dolls, feeding and loving them, just like my mom did taking care of all of us kids. She always made it look so easy and always kept a smile on her face, even when times were hard. Sometimes a good parent and teacher like my mom cannot prepare you for some things life can throw your way.

My mother taught me so many things in life from showing me how to care about someone to learning how to throw a football, so I could play with the boys. We often went fishing or swimming, but one thing for sure was that when the street lights came on it was time to get home. She taught me how to take care of myself.

Then the day came! I became a mother. It was a great joy in my life to look down at his precious face and I knew that he was mine to love and raise. As time went on and time flew by, I soon realized I was a mother of five: two boys and three girls. They sure kept me busy, chasing them in every direction with laughs and giggles the entire way. Then my life changed.

On a mid-spring day, a few months after my baby daughter's first birthday, that's when it happened. My world and life turned completely upside down. Nothing or no one could have prepared me for that day. I lost my daughter. I was devastated and didn't understand. I carried her for nine months, watched her learn to crawl, and she was starting to walk and go everywhere. Then, in the blink of an eye, she lost her life. She was only sixteen months old when it happened. To this day, I still can't bring myself to talk about what happened.

Sadly, instead of me having time to grieve, I had to put my feelings on the back burner. I had four other children and a husband that needed my love and support. I had to be the strong one and keep them going. I made peace with it the best I could and kept my head held up for them. I had to be the tough one and be the shoulder to cry on. My oldest daughter now suffers from P.T.S.D. and has night terror induced seizures as a result.

I just want everyone to love and cherish their children. Every child born is a special gift. Every moment spent with your child, whether it be good or bad, should be cherished. In the blink of an eye everything could change. You won't have hugs or kisses anymore, or even little arguments. Don't live life with doubt and fear; just get out there and love every minute of life with your children. You never know when it might be your last.

Jamie Wilkes
© 2017
American

Gujarati To English

ભારતના તહેવારો

તહેવારો જીવન ઉજવણી છે બધા દેશના ધાર્મિક અને સાંસ્કૃતિક તહેવારો છે. ભારતીય તહેવારો અસંખ્ય છે તેઓ મજા અને રંગીન છે તેઓ અમારા વ્યસ્ત જીવનમાં આનંદ અને શાંતિ લાવે છે. ભારતીય તહેવારોને ત્રણ શ્રેણીઓમાં વહેંચી શકાય છે. રાજકીય, ધાર્મિક અને મોસમી મોટાભાગના ભારતીય તહેવારો પાસે તેમના ધર્મ કારણો છે. કેટલાક ખૂબ જ આદરણીય પુરુષો, અને સ્ત્રીઓ અને તેમની યાદશક્તિ સાથે જોડાયેલા છે, અને કેટલાક નવા સીઝનનું સ્વાગત કરે છે. રાષ્ટ્રીય તહેવારો જેવી કે સ્વતંત્રતા દિવસ, પ્રજાસત્તાક દિવસ, ગાંધી જયંતિ રાષ્ટ્રીય રજાઓ તરીકે જાહેર કરવામાં આવી છે. તેઓ ઉત્સાહ અને રાષ્ટ્રીય ગર્વ સાથે સમગ્ર દેશમાં ઉજવવામાં આવે છે. અને, આપણે આપણા સૈનિકોને પણ યાદ રાખીએ છીએ કે જેઓ આપણા દેશની સ્વતંત્રતા માટે તેમના જીવનનો બલિદાન આપે છે. નવી દિલ્હી, રીપબ્લિક ડે પર સૌથી વધુ ભવ્ય પરેડમાંની એક છે.

દિવાળી ઉત્સવ છે તે હિંદુઓનો સૌથી મોટો તહેવાર છે. ચૌદ વર્ષનું દેશનિકાલ પછી તે ભગવાન રામની અયોધ્યામાં પરત ફરતા ચિહ્ન તરીકે ચિહ્નિત થયેલ છે. અયોધ્યાના લોકોએ મીણબત્તીઓ પ્રગટ કરીને અને તેમના ગામમાં સજાવટ કરીને ભગવાન રામનું સ્વાગત કર્યું. દિવાળીનો

તહેવાર પાંચ સતત દિવસ માટે ઉજવવામાં આવે છે. લોકો મીણબત્તીઓ, ફટાકડા કરવા, ભેટોનું આદાન-પ્રદાન કરીને ઉજવે છે.

દેવી દુર્ગાના નવ જુદા સ્વરૂપોની ભક્તિ કરવા માટે નવરાત્રીનો ઉત્સવ ઉજવાય છે. ઘણા ઉત્સાહ અને ખુશી સાથે નવ દિવસ ઉજવાય છે. ઘણા ભક્તો નવ દિવસ માટે ઉપવાસ કરે છે. તેથી, ઘણા સ્થળોએ, લોકો ભેગા અને જૂથોમાં દાંદિયા અને ગરબા નૃત્ય કરે છે. નવરાત્રીના દસમા દિવસને દશેરા કહેવામાં આવે છે.

હોળી રંગનો તહેવાર છે. તે દુષ્ટ પર સારી વચ્ચે વિજય દર્શાવે છે હોળીકાહાન (એક મોટી હાફકા) કરીને હોળીની શરૂઆત પહેલાં ઉજવણી રાતે શરૂ થાય છે. લોકો અગ્નિની સામે ધાર્મિક વિધિઓ કરે છે, અને તેઓ પ્રાર્થના કરે છે કે તેમની આંતરિક દુષ્ટતા હોલીકાના માર્ગનો નાશ કરે છે, જે રાક્ષસ રાજાની બહેન છે, જેમાં હોલીકા બળી હતી. બીજા દિવસે લોકો રંગો દ્વારા જીવન ભેગા અને ઉજવણી કરે છે.

ભારત મારું ઘર છે, અને તહેવારો ઉજવવા માટે આ એક સુંદર સ્થળ છે. જો તમને ક્યારેય ત્યાં જવાની તક મળી હોય, તો ભારતના સૌથી આનંદપ્રદ અને યાદગાર તહેવારોમાંના એકનો લાભ લેવા અને તેનો લાભ લેવાની ખાતરી કરો.

Komal Patel
© 2017
Indian

India's Festivals

Festivals are a celebration of life. All nations have their religious and cultural festivals. Indian festivals are numerous. They are fun and colorful. They bring joy and peace to our busy life.

Indian festivals can be divided in three categories: Political, religious, and seasonal. Most Indian festivals are juxtaposed with religious customs. Some are connected with very respectable men and women, and their historical leaders, and some are to welcome new seasons.

National festivals like The Independence Day, The Republic Day, and Gandhi Jayanti have been declared as national holidays. They are celebrated in the whole country with lots of enthusiasm and national pride. And, we also remember our soldiers who sacrificed their lives for the freedom of our country. Our capital, New Delhi, witnesses one of the most majestic parades ever on Republic Day.

Diwali is a festival of lights. It is one of the biggest festivals of Hindus. It is marked as Lord Ram's return to Ayodhya after fourteen years of exile. People of Ayodhya welcomed Lord Ram by lighting candles and decorating their village. The festival of Diwali is celebrated for five continuous days. People celebrate it by lighting candles, doing fireworks, exchanging gifts, etc.

Festival of Navratri is celebrated to worship nine different forms of the goddess Durga. It is celebrated for nine days with lots of enthusiasm and happiness. Many devotees do fasting for nine days. So, in many places, people gather and do Dandiya and garba dance in groups. The tenth day of Navratri is called Dussehra.

Holi is a festival of colors. It signifies a victory between good over evil. The celebration starts the night before Holi begins by doing Holika Dahan (a large bonfire). People perform rituals in front of the bonfire, and they pray that their internal evil destroys the way of Holika, who is the sister of the demon king, in which Holika was burned. The next day people gather and celebrate life through colors.

India is my home country, and it is a lovely place to celebrate festivals. If you ever get a chance to go there, be sure to visit and take advantage of one of India's most enjoyable and memorable festivals.

Komal Patel

Indian

Spanish To English

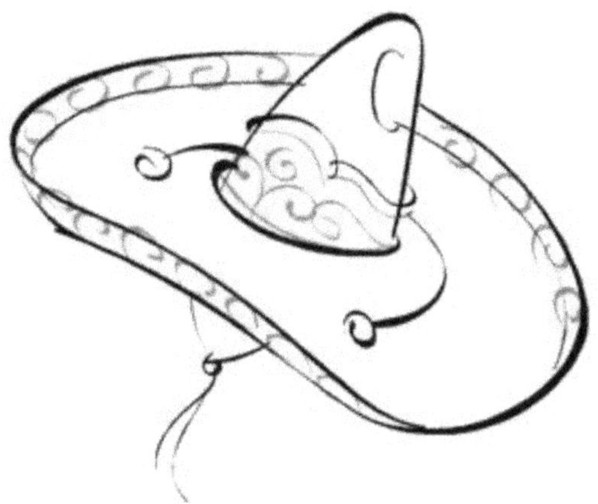

La Leyenda de la Llorona

Había una vez, una mujer muy hermosa, indígena de México que se enamoró con un hombre extranjero que venía de España. Tuvieron un hermoso noviazgo. Se casaron y tuvieron tres hijos, una hermosa niña y dos niños. Sus vidas transcurrieron muy normales hasta que el hombre tuvo que regresar a su país. Ella lo esperaba con mucho amor.

Finalmente, el regresó a México con una mala noticia. Se había casado en España con una hermosa princesa y que solo regresó a México para llevarse a sus hijos. Llorando enloquecida por el dolor, la madre de los niños le pidió a su esposo de no llevarlos de ella. El trató de hablar con su suegro, pero sin suerte.

Ella tomó a sus tres hijos y salió de su casa. Se fueron caminando por el pueblo, pasando campos, subieron a lo alto de una montaña, hasta que encontraron un rio muy ancho. Ahí, a la orilla del rio ahogó a sus hijos. Cuando su esposo y sus padres la encontraron era demasiado tarde. Los niños estaban muertos. Ella quiso matarse porque su dolor era tan grande. Pero, el Dios le dijo que no podría descansar ni encontrar consuelo hasta que ella encuentre a sus hijos y les entregará a Dios. Dios ya tenía a los niños con El, pero quiso castigarla a vagar por toda la eternidad buscando sin éxito a sus hijos.

La leyenda de la llorona se cuenta cuando es una noche muy obscura o con tormenta, cuando uno está al lado de un rio, un lago, o el mar. Se dice que aparece una mujer gritando, "hay mis hijos", y que está tratando de robar a los niños. También la leyenda dice que cuando la llorona encuentra hombres que están muy tomados y quieren tener sexo con ella, ella toma venganza por lo que su esposo le hizo, se convierte en un horrible monstro y les grita, "HAY MIS HIJOS." Les saca los ojos, a otros las matas y a los que han quedados vivos los sigue espantado todas las noches hasta que se enloquecen con su espantoso grito, “hay mis hijos”.

Entonces, hay que tener mucho cuidado si se le aparece una mujer muy hermosa a medianoche. Puede ser la llorona, y su grito de “hay mis hijos” le puede enloquecer. Esto no es un cuento es una historia real que mi abuelita me contó cuando yo era niña.

Yenny Sanchez

Mexican

The Crying Woman

Once upon a time, there was a beautiful indigenous woman from Mexico. She fell in love with a foreigner from Spain. They had a beautiful relationship. They married soon after and had three children. They had a lovely daughter and two handsome sons. Their lives continued, and it was a very normal life until the man had to return to his country. She waited patiently for him to return and was filled with much love for him.

Finally, he returned to Mexico with some bad news. He had married another woman in Spain, and she was a beautiful princess. He had only returned to Mexico to gather his children. She cried out in pain, the mother of her children would be lost to her husband, never to see them again. He tried to speak to his father-in-law about the situation, but without luck he never spoke to him.

She took her three children and left home. They went running toward the town, passing farms, and then climbing to the top of a mountain, until they encountered a large river. There, at the border of the river, she drowned her children. When her husband and her parents found her, it was too late. The children were dead. She tried to kill herself because the pain was so great. But God told her that she would never rest nor find consolation until she found her children. However, God had already taken her children with him. But he wanted to punish her and to roam for all of eternity while searching for her children without success.

The Crying Woman Legend is often told on a dark stormy night when people are standing near a river, a lake, or ocean. It is said that she will appear screaming, "There are my children." Also, she will try to steal children away from families. The legend says that when the crying woman encounters men that they will drink a lot and want to have sex with her. She takes her revenge on them as she would have done to her husband. She converts into a horrible monster and screams at them, "THERE ARE MY CHILDREN." She cuts out the men's eyes, and then quietly kills them. Every night she searches for her children while constantly crying, "There are my children." So, everyone needs to take much care if they encounter the crying woman if she appears during the middle of the night. She might appear as a beautiful woman, and if she does, it might be the llorona screaming, "There are my children." She will drive you crazy. This is the story that my grandmother used to tell me as a little girl.

Yenny Sanchez
© 2017
Mexican

Caminar Con Dios

Estoy caminando con Dios
En la mañana lluviosa
Y el sol brillante es hermoso
el sonido más lindo
son los pájaros cantores.
Los pájaros me hablan
Y mientras es una mañana para tomar
Un chocolate caliente
Y mi cuerpo se siente fuerte y estoy
Listo para adorar a mi Dios
Estoy caminando en medio de mis rosas
Y Dios me presenta con su gloria
Y me siento más tranquilo
Recibir gotas de sus regalos

Fabiola Sanchez
© 2017
Mexicana

Walking with God

I'm walking with God
in the rainy morning.
The bright sun is beautiful.
The best sound to hear is the
singing birds.
The birds are talking to me.
It's a morning to drink
hot chocolate.
My body feels strong.
I am ready to worship my God.
I'm walking in the middle of my roses.
God presents me with his glorious wonders,
and I feel calmer while receiving his gifts.

Fabiola Sanchez

Mexican

Vida Agrícola del Pueblo Hispano

Buenos Días, mi nombre es Saúl, y vivo en Carolina del norte. Me crecí en la pequeña aldea llamada Tecozautla, Hidalgo, México. Yo les ayudaba a mis padres en la agricultura. Sin embargo, la vida en México era muy dura porque no teníamos las máquinas para hacer el trabajo como lo hacemos hoy en los Estados Unidos. Todo fue hecho por caballos arando la tierra o por el sudor de nuestro cuerpo. Al final del día, siempre teníamos dolor de espalda por estar agachados todo el día o de levantar objetos pesados. Siempre soñé de cómo sería la vida con el uso de la tecnología ayudándome a mí y a mi familia.

Hoy en día, me subo a los árboles para ganarme la vida, y la tecnología ha sido útil en mi oficio como jardinero. La tecnología en América ha incorporado máquinas como tractores, camiones para acarreo y sistemas automáticos de irrigación. Se podría pensar que un país como México tendría este tipo de equipo. El pueblo estadounidense da por cuenta que las máquinas pueden hacer todo el trabajo. Todos los países no son creados iguales cuando se trata de la distribución del trabajo.

Los hombres y las mujeres hispanas trabajan con sus manos y espaldas. Comienzan antes de que el sol salga y trabajan después de que el sol se cae. De joven, teníamos que cultivar cacahuates como parte de nuestra cosecha. Esta era una cosecha de dinero para nosotros para sobrevivir durante los meses del invierno. Esta fue una planta extremadamente dura para sembrar y cosechar. Primeramente, la tierra se necesitaba arar con caballo o con las manos, espalda y azadón. Los cacahuates se sembraban en parcelas de una acre. Después, se quitaba la mala hierba alrededor de cada planta con las manos. Yo tenía que sacar las malas hierbas cubeta por cubeta a mano y se las daba a las gallinas, vacas y las cabras. Si el tiempo era seco y caliente, teníamos que excavar zanjas del manar hacia cada hila de cacahuates para darles agua. Cuando era tiempo de cosechar, las plantas se sacaban de la tierra con un caballo y arado. Yo seguía atrás del caballo levantando las nueces y los metía en una bolsa con cupo de 50 libras. Luego los poníamos en la asotea de la casa para secar por 2 o 3 días. Cuando los cacahuates se habían secado, los empaquetamos y los llevamos al mercado. El precio era equivalente a veinte dólares americanos.

Así, como puede ver el lector, la tecnología puede ser muy beneficiosa para el pueblo hispano. La agricultura no es fácil para ninguna cultura. Sin embargo, la agricultura para las personas que carecen de tecnología es el doble de difícil debido a las limitaciones de la obra a mano en su lugar. Por lo tanto, la próxima vez que usted está comiendo algunos cacahuates salados de la compañía "Planter's Peanut Company", recuerde que fueron cosechados en las espaldas de granjeros hispanos.

Saul Castillo Hernandez

Mexicano

Farm Life of the Hispanic People

Buenos dias, my name is Saul, and I live in North Carolina. I grew up in small country village called Tecozautla Hidalgo, Mexico. I used to help my parents on the farm. However, life in Mexico was very hard because we did not have the machines to do the work like we have today in the United States. Everything was done by horses pulling plows or by the sweat of our brows. We always had very sore backs from bending over or lifting heavy objects by the end of the day. I always dreamed of what life would look like in America with the use of technology helping me and my family.

Today, I climb trees for a living, and technology has been useful in my trade and in my life as a gardener. Technology in America has incorporated machines like tractors, trucks for hauling, and automatic irrigation systems. You would think that a country like Mexico would have these types of equipment in place. American people take it for granted that machines can do all the work. All countries are not created equal when it comes to the distribution of labor.

Hispanic men and women work with their hands and backs. They start before the sun comes up and work after the sun goes down. As a young boy, we would have to grow peanuts as part of our crops. This was a money crop for us to survive during the winter months. This was an extremely hard plant to sow and harvest. First, each row would have to be trenched out either by a horse and plow or by hands, back, and hoe. Peanuts were planted in one-acre plots of land. Then, the weeding would be done around each plant with the weed being pulled out by hand. I would have to carry the weeds out one bucket at a time. I would feed the chickens, cows, and goats. If the weather was dry and hot, we would have to dig trenches from the well to each row of peanuts to water the plants. When it came time to harvest the plants, the peanuts would have to be dug up with the horse and plow. I would follow behind gathering the nuts, and I would put them in 50 lb. tote bags, and then we would dry them on the roof of the house for 2-3 days. After the peanuts had dried, we would bag them up and take them to the local market. The price was equivalent to twenty American dollars.

So, as the reader can see, technology can be quite beneficial for the Hispanic people. Farming is not easy for any culture. However, farming for people who lack technology is twice as difficult because of the labor constraints put into place. Therefore, the next time you are eating some salted peanuts from Planter's peanut company, remember, it was grown on the backs of Hispanic farmers.

Saul Castillo Hernandez
© 2017
Mexican

A Journey of Faith

My story begins with no hope, no heart, and all pride. However, by end of the story, it is my earnest desire you will know the fullness of my life that has occurred in this country. Most beginnings do not start so lost, but mine does. I started this journey as an immigrant, but I ended as a citizen. I was born in Yuriria, Mexico on the tenth of September 1983 to my mother Maria Luz and my father Gonzalo Martinez. I was the second oldest boy. My brother Miguel is three years older than I am. I have three sisters that are all younger. Our small single room home held four family members. My mother raised me mostly due to my father being absent most of my childhood. It is common in Mexico for this to happen as a majority of Mexico's men depart for America once they are old enough to start families. Poverty, as in most countries, breeds a society greedy for money it does not have. It is common for young boys to assume they must go to America and work to support their families in Mexico or became involved in drug rings and gangs. We all attended a grade school as children but quickly learned in the home that 'cash is king' and education holds little value or promise.

In 1998, I decided I was old enough to begin financially supporting my family. I was only fourteen when I made my trip to America with my older brother. My brother and I crossed the border several times over the course of several years. Each time was a challenge, and some even died attempting it!

Working in America gave me a great sense of pride. I enjoyed being able to send money home to my mother and even getting the chance to help rebuild my family's home. My days were spent working, sometimes two or three jobs; my nights were spent entertaining ideas of becoming rich. I did not attend any school throughout my teenage and young adult years. I did not need to according to my upbringing. I lived as a wild and lonely youth; but, as long as those checks were cashed, I was urged to press onward.

As I grew up in America, I became bilingual and that opened even more doors for a deeper, sinful, empty life. I eventually decided to involve others in my misery and became involved with a woman I later married and had two children with. Living selfishly motivated turmoil and the marriage ended in divorce. The abrupt separation left me alone with my two children in poverty. Everything I had fought not to become happened. It was hard for me to understand why I could not fix matters with my own determination and money. I had always been under the belief that hard work and courage could overcome all obstacles, even my own failures. After a month of struggling to feed my children and myself, a wonderful act of kindness occurred which changed everything! I had already been attending a church, believing that going through the motions of Christianity would help me and my children. However, what I was expecting and what actually happened opened my eyes forever. I and my children, had gone a few days without food when a random stranger came to my house and anonymously dropped off food. I could not believe it! Why would someone I did not know and not wanting credit to do this? I was expecting money and aid from the people who knew me and heard my complaints. Instead, this came from a complete stranger.

From this, I began to learn that my outward acts and easy beliefs were not faith. But something more changed between God and me after that. For months, I found myself studying God's word and seeking saving faith. Sometime, into my journey, God found me… and my search was not a search at all but more like a blind man looking for a light switch that was there all along! The new desires placed in me guided me to baptism late summer 2009. So much knowledge and understanding filled my days. I learned about the church's history, the early reformers, and evangelism. My mind was flooded with theology and doctrines that inspired me and my new walk in faith.

Teachings such as total depravity, unconditional election, limited atonement, irresistible grace, and perseverance of the saints filled my head. Everything I thought I knew, I quickly threw out and began depending on "solo Scriptura," scripture alone, to guide my life. Advice from men no longer satisfied me, and I became hungry for God. Things have changed so much since then. I met my new wife, whose faith is equally yoked with my own. We, together, with God, have raised a "blended" family. We struggle each day but somehow the burden seems light. Our children have been taught to be a family even though bloodlines do not tie us together. Now, I have been given a new hope.

While politically, America and Mexico are at odds, I have found that all cultures have struggled with immigration. I have also learned that no one has ever gotten it right! I no longer want my value and worth to be determined by a country or a culture. I've decided none of these things move me in my spirit. Instead, now, I desire to obey this country's leaders and behoove myself to their demands. I desire now to care more for others than myself. I believe that God will give me a way to wisely express my love for this country and its people in due time. My citizenship may never come in America but I promise you I have already become a citizen of the kingdom of God and that is all one ever really needs. AMEN!

Jose Jesus Martinez Sandoval
© 2017
Hispanic

Life Is…

Life is beauty,
You have to admire.
Life is a dream,
It comes true.
Life is a challenge,
You have to face.
Life is a game,
You have to know
how to play to win.
Life is a promise
You have to keep.
Life is a joy,
You have to laugh.
Life is a pain,
You have to heal.
Life is a song,
You have to listen.
Life is a reality,
You have to live.

Etbaruc G. Vazquez
© 2017
Mexican

La Historia de Mi Puebla

Hola, es Yesika. Esta es la historia de mi pueblo. Mis abuelos me contaron como fue fundada y porque lo llamaron Salinas de Hidalgo. Es interesante para mí saber la historia del lugar donde yo nací y viví de joven.

La población que hoy es Salinas de Hidalgo, en el estado de San Luis Potosí, fue fundada el 8 de septiembre, 1596, por el conquistador Juan de Tolosa. El nombre del pueblo era entonces Salinas del Penon Blanco. Recibió su nombre debido a las salinas que se encuentran en el lugar y que hasta la fecha se minan comercialmente para la explotación de la sal.

El 24 de febrero de 1811, llegó a Salinas Don Miguel Hidalgo y Costilla, que se retiraba a Texas después de la Batalla del Puente de Calderón. Miguel Hidalgo se sirvió por unas horas en Salinas, en la casa grande de la negociación salinera construida en las afueras de la ciudad. Esta casa estaba rodeada por un muro defensivo, porque Salinas sufría continuos ataques de grupos de indígenas que no se querían someterse al gobierno. Algunos de mis ancestros estaban en ataques contra el gobierno.

El 29 de septiembre de 1960, el congreso de San Luis Potosí cambió el nombre de mi pueblo a Salinas de Hidalgo, en honor al padre del país, Miguel Hidalgo y Costilla.

Yesika Valenciano
© 2017
Mexicana

The History of My Town

Hi, my name is Yesika. This is the story of my town. My grandparents told me how it was founded and why it was called Salinas de Hidalgo. It is interesting for me to know about the place where I was born and lived in my youth.

The town that today is Salinas de Hidalgo, in the state of San Luis Potosi, was founded on September 8, 1596, by the conqueror Juan de Tolosa. The town's name at that time was Salinas del Penon Blanco (Salt of the White Stone). It received its name due to the salt flats that are in that place and to this date are mined commercially for the exploitation of salt.

On February 24, 1811, Don Miguel Hidalgo y Costilla, arrived in Salinas as he was retreating to Texas after the Battle of Puente de Calderon. Miguel Hidalgo stayed for a few hours in Salinas, in the large house of the salt mine built on the outskirts of the town. This house was surrounded by a defensive wall because Salinas suffered continuous attacks by groups of indigenous people who did not want to submit themselves to the government. Some of my ancestors were in the attacks on the government.

On September 29, 1960, the congress of San Luis Potosi changed the name of my town to Salinas de Hidalgo, in honor of the father of the country, Miguel Hidalgo y Costilla.

Yesika Valenciano
© 2017
Mexican

Hasta Que te Conocí

La Chica del Autobús/La Chica Fría y El Chico Romántico

Este es un pequeño relato de mi adolescencia, el cual ocurrió unos años atrás, el día que conocí a una bella dama que me cambió la vida desde aquí a la luna literalmente hablando, una historia de alegría, risas, tristeza y esperanza.

Era una mañana bastante soleada había un excelente clima ese día era mi primer día de escuela en un país diferente y con un idioma nuevo el cual todavía no lo hablaba. Mis padres me inscribieron en esta escuela secundaria la cual para llegar tomaba aproximadamente treinta minutos en autobús. El día llegó el tan anhelado lunes ya estaba ahí. Ese día me sentí un poco nervioso, era una escuela nueva con personas que no conocía. Me levanté temprano para tomar el autobús escolar, esperé veinte minutos y la verdad se me hicieron eternos. Unos instantes después llego el autobús, para mi sorpresa, yo era el único estudiante el cual lo abordaría.

Entré al autobús a mi parecer había demasiados extraños y pocos lugares disponibles para sentarse, pero en la parte de atrás del autobús, una sonrisa hermosa y unos ojos tan fijos me estaban viendo. Ella solo sonrió y yo también lo hice. Si ese sería mi lugar no solo hasta que llegara a la escuela, sino que hasta que tuviera que despedirme de ella y sin darme cuenta que ella sería una de mis mejores amigas y que hasta la trataría como parte de mi familia. En ese momento me sentí muy tenso, había tantas cosas para hablar con esta dama y ninguna se me ocurrían. Pero unos minutos después todo cambió. Creo que hablamos y reímos demasiado y hasta sentí que la conocía de toda la vida. El tiempo pasó tan rápido y finalmente llegamos a una escuela muy grande con demasiadas personas. En ese momento me pregunte ¿ahora adónde voy? Lo bueno es que había conocido a alguien que ya había asistido muchas veces a este lugar. Si la chica del autobús y para mi sorpresa la primera de mis siete clases estaría con ella.

Baje del autobús seguimos charlando mientras caminábamos por los pasillos de este nuevo lugar para mí, pero a la vez un lugar muy atrayente e interesante. A unos pasos antes de entrar al salón de clases fue cuando la vi, "wow" vaya que me quedé impresionado con solo verla. Si la belleza se definiera con una sola palabra entonces no sabría cual usar para describirla. Era increíble como tanta belleza podría caber en sus escasos cinco pies de altura. Sin pensarlo en ese momento me acerqué a ella, sentí un pequeño escalofrío recorriendo mi cuerpo, en ese momento ella volteó y me vio. La verdad me sentí tan vulnerable. Sentí como que si su mirada pudiera haber atravesado mi alma y ver en ella todas esas emociones que sentí por ella con solo verla. Me acerqué y le pregunté "¿Sabes qué hora es?" Valla introducción "ja ja ja" no se me pudo haber ocurrido algo más original. Ella solo sonrío, en ese momento sentí que me derretí como un helado a unos noventa y ocho grados de calor a las doce del día con solo estar frente a ella.

Converse con ella por unos minutos ella también estaría en mi primera clase. Me dejo tan impresionado no solo por ser tan guapa, si no por su manera de pensar. También tenía un sentido del humor fatal igual al mío. Bueno al parecer teníamos algo en común. Los minutos pasaban y ella más me atraía. Eran tan amable, tan hermosa, tan frágil, pero tan fuerte que con tan solo escuchar su voz daba esperanzas a cualquiera que la escuchara incluyéndome a mi claro.

El día había pasado tan rápido y recuerdo que había tomado aproximadamente siete clases diferentes y ya quería que fuera martes para poder verla otra vez. Tan joven y tan iluso creía que podía conquistar el mundo entero, pero yo quería conquistar su corazón. Al fin llego el tan anhelado día martes. Esa misma mañana recuerdo haberme levantado más temprano para así poder tener más tiempo y así poder arreglarme mejor para así poder llamar la atención de esta bella dama, que me tenía loco con tanta ilusión de conocerla y así poder saber más de ella.

Esa misma mañana apenas bajando del autobús con mi amiga pude ver el autobús de ella llegando. También valla mi sorpresa cuando vi a este joven abrazándola y hasta la besó en la frente. Ella tampoco se molestó. En ese momento me sentí muy raro, puede que estaba empezando a tener celos, pero porque celos si apenas la había conocido. Sin pensarlo ya me estaba mintiendo a mí mismo. Luego en la primera clase estaba hablando con mi amiga. la chica del autobús, esa amiga incondicional, la primera que conocí mi primer día de escuela la que estaría conmigo en las buenas y en las malas. Recuerdo que estábamos bromeando con otro amigo, en ese momento le dije, sabes que te puedo hacer una pregunta, ella respondió si, conoces a él joven que estaba abrazando a Kayla. Ese era el nombre de la chica la cual me tenía tan enamorado y ella respondió si, él es el hermano de Kayla, Que sorpresa era esta que me quede pensando por varios minutos. Me sentí tonto por tener aquel pensamiento tan inmaduro, pero a la misma vez me sentí muy bien porque había una posibilidad de expresar mis sentimientos a esta dama.

Así la semana pasó y cada día mis emociones se hacían más fuertes por esta extraña de baja altura, una sonrisa encantadora y un hermoso cabello, la cual llegó en un momento inesperado pero muy bueno a la vez. Si me hubieran preguntado qué era lo que más me atraía de esta hermosa dama, yo diría que "me quedaría con todo." Lo bueno y malo, lo alegre y lo triste, su mal sentido del humor y su bella sonrisa, sus celos y su amor, en fin, algo así como la perfección en persona. Eso era lo que mi tonto corazón sentía cada vez que la miraba. Llego el viernes, el momento de la despedida llego, pero lo bueno es que la volvería a ver el lunes otra vez.

Ese primer fin de semana me pareció eterno cada minuto y segundo pasaban tan lento, y eso que era la primera semana que la había conocido. El tan anhelado lunes llego y con el llego el valor y la esperanza de poder decirle lo que mi corazón sentía por ella. No sabría decir de dónde pude sacar el valor de decirle que me gustaba en el momento que la vi, le dije todo lo que estaba sintiendo por ella hasta con detalles. Ella solo sonrió me vio tan fijamente, como haber olvidado esa mirada tan directa y penetrante que aún después de tantos años la recuerdo como si fuera ayer. Luego de unos segundos todo cambió el bello momento, cuando ella dijo que no estaba prepara para una relación en ese momento, yo me sentí muy decepcione me dije para que tantas ilusiones y bellas emociones.

Fui tan tonto en pensar esas cosas tan egoístamente solo en mí. Los días pasaron y todavía no la podía sacar de mi cabeza. Me pregunté a mí mismo porque esa actitud si cuando la vi y le dije lo que estaba sintiendo su reacción fue tan notoria, su actitud la delataba, su carita, sus ojos y todo su cuerpo me decían todo lo contrario. Mi cabeza estaba dando vueltas. Me pregunté a mí mismo que hice mal o en que fallé. Yo sabía que no era el único chico que estaba enamorado de ella. También había dos personas más que andaban soñando en las nubes por ella, bueno ya serian tres conmigo. Aun siendo estos chicos físicamente mejor que mí, ellos tampoco pudieron lograr lo que yo también quería. Uno de ellos era más alto y más fuerte físicamente, él otro parecía un galán de telenovela, tenía un buen sentido del humor y era difícil no reír cuando estaba alrededor.

Yo también tenía lo mío, si es cierto no estaba tan alto tampoco parecía galán de telenovela, en fin algo así como ese producto en descuento del cual se querían deshacer rápido, lo bueno es que yo era más amable con ella, la escuchaba. Le daba esperanzas y si tuviera algo en lo que tampoco entendiera también trataba de ayudarla, aunque al final era a mí al que terminaba ayudando. También yo era más romántico con ella, no sé si eso es una virtud o un defecto en mí, recuerdo como se sonrojaba su carita cuando le dedicaba un poema o una canción. Lo bueno es que conmigo era diferente, se podría decir que había una conexión.

Una mañana estaba hablando con mi amiga sobre ella, pero en mi mente todavía tenía aquel pensamiento de porque me rechazo. Pero en mi mente tenía el pensamiento que eso no era un rechazo y en eso surgió el tema, mi amiga ya sabía lo que yo había hecho y le pregunte, "¿Sabes porque Kayla es así? Yo le declare mis sentimientos y estoy casi seguro que ella quería decir que sí." Mi amiga respondió a mi pregunta. "Hace dos años Kayla conoció a un joven, así como tú, muy amable y romántico con ella. Ellos se hicieron novios y sinceramente se veían muy felices hasta que un día ella lo encontró besándose con su mejor amiga. Desde ese entonces ella es así más fría, precavida, y no confía mucho en las personas especialmente los chicos." Esta era la parte de la historia que yo no conocía. Tan bella y tan amable, pero a veces tan fría, con tanto dolor en su corazón y sin poder expresarlo con palabras aun cuando lo hubiera querido. Termino la clase, yo estaba afuera esperándola, sentí que tenía que decirle algo. Ella tenía que sentir que no estaba sola, que aun cuando todos se marcharan yo iba a estar ahí para ella desde ahora y hasta el final. No me importo quien estuviera a mi alrededor. Cuando la vi mi cuerpo actúo por si solo y sin pensarlo dos veces la abrasé tan fuerte y sentí que no la quería dejar ir. Ese era el lugar donde ella pertenecía. Después de un breve momento de tenerla en mis brazos, le susurre al oído diciendo que iba esperarla y que prefería esperar días, meses o aún más tiempo que vivir esta vida tan solitaria sin ella a mi lado. La sonrisa que me dio después de haberla visto sonreír tantas veces esa sonrisa era muy diferente a las anteriores, en ese instante me dieron tantas gansas de robarle un beso, pero entendí que no era un buen momento y que tenía que ser paciente y esperar.

Conforme el verano se iba se aproximaba el invierno, pero ni ese frío de invierno podía apagar o enfriar todas esas emociones que sentía por ella. Sentí que los días pasaban más rápido y Kayla y yo nos hacíamos más inseparables. También la chica del autobús andaba con nosotros, éramos algo como los tres mosqueteros de la secundaria. Nosotros nos escapábamos los fines de semana para disfrutar de aquellos días de adolescencia. Ese mismo viernes decidimos que iríamos a la playa el sábado, ósea el día siguiente. Yo dije está bien, pero en mi mente había otra preocupación. Me dije que el agua está muy helada y será que me veré bien en traje de baño. Bueno ellas se verán increíbles, pero yo creo que me veré como un espagueti con pantalones. Pero si es por ellas creo que puedo aguantar esto. Por fin el sábado estaba ahí y no me equivoque, se veían magnificas, pero que buena suerte la mía ese día tenía una temperatura súper buena. El sol alumbraba con todo hasta las diez de la mañana. Luego se puso muy helado, y yo que no me llevo muy bien con el frío me quede sentado en la arena viéndolas divertirse. Envuelto en mi toalla, estuvimos ahí todo el día y al final nos llevamos un buen momento. Disfrutamos mucho los tres ya caminando de vuelta a casa creo que Kayla nado demasiado y andaba súper cansada yo le dije que la cargaría. Al principio no quería, pero creo que la convencí la cargué en mi espalda hasta que llegamos. Admito que ya no podía más, pero me aguanté, lo pude lograr gracias a ella.

Primero llegamos a su casa, sus padres estaban ahí, en eso se vino una lluvia muy fuerte, bueno en Florida casi siempre es así. De ese día tan especial, los tres obtuvimos algo más que un maravilloso día, un resfriado. La lluvia estaba muy fuerte y había muchos relámpagos. Sus padres me pidieron que pasara la noche ahí con ellos que era muy peligroso salir por la tormenta. Para nuestra suerte ese día estaba pasando un huracán por este estado, yo no estaba para nada disgustado. Al contrario, pasar todo el día con ellas estaba súper bien y ahora un ratito en la noche con ellas. Vimos una película, que más podría haber pedido, así cuando la película se acabó solo nosotros tres estábamos despiertos. Yo me quedaría en el sillón, ella y la chica del autobús en su cuarto. Las acompañé a su cuarto cuando me estaba despidiendo dándole las buenas noches me di la vuelta en ese momento y ella me abrazo. La verdad que no me pude resistir y me di la vuelta y la besé. Ella no se disgustó. Esta vez yo no tuve que decir que si quería ser mi novia, ella me pregunto si yo quería ser su novio. En ese momento sentí como que si estuviera soñando. Aun después de tantas cosas que pase no sabía si esto iba a funcionar, al fin la tengo aquí conmigo y poder escuchar esto de sus labios. Me sentí súper bien, al fin había paz en mi corazón.

El día domingo la pasamos juntos, esta vez solo ella y yo. Tan rápido se nos fue el día. Llegó otro lunes, pero esta vez caminábamos de la mano por los pasillos de la escuela. Vi a los dos jóvenes que también estaban interesados en ella, me quedaron viendo con una mirada fija. En mi mente decía, "Lo siento caballeros, la diferencia es que yo nací para ella y eso nadie me lo quita mientras yo viva en su corazón y mientras ella me quiera." Cada día me sentía más bien, más vivo con ella como que si pudiera morir y volver nacer con ella.

La navidad se acercaba y otro sábado estábamos planeando salir a bailar con todos los de la clase. El plan se hizo dos días antes, la razón es que ese sería el último año que la clase estaría junta. El siguiente año muchos se irían de esta escuela y otros estarían en otras clases incluyéndome. Cada día Kayla sonreía más y más sinceramente. Eso era toda mi felicidad solo con una simple expresión en su carita ni se imaginaba las cosas que le hacía a mi corazón. Un día antes del baile me enseño su vestido. Lo acababa de comprar. Ella dijo. “Espero que te guste, lo compre pensando en ti.” Mientras yo la besaba ella solo sonreía. Ese día yo la esperaría en el baile y ella llegaría con mi mejor amiga la chica del autobús. Estuve esperando por unos cuarenta minutos y pensé creo que se arregló de más y se le hizo un poco tarde. Eso es lo que quería pensar. Los minutos pasaban y más me preocupaba. Llame a su casa, pero sus padres dijeron que no sabían dónde estaba. Al final ella nunca llego, hubo un accidente, un conductor en estado de ebriedad se pasó la luz roja y las impacto. Ella murió antes de llegar al hospital.

Aproximadamente diez minutos después recibí una llamada de su padre. Me dijo que ellas estaban en el hospital y que todavía no sabían cuál era el motivo el cual ellas estuvieran en ese lugar. Yo quería pensar que todo estaba bien y que no era algo grave. Llegué como loco, muy alterado al hospital preguntando por ellas. Entonces llegó una enfermera y me llevo hacia esta habitación donde se encontraban. Primero vi a mi mejor amiga, ella tenía un brazo muy golpeado estaba un poco morado y tenía unas cuantas pequeñas cortadas. Lo bueno es que iba a estar buen. Luego me llevaron a esta otra habitación. Cuando entre pude ver una parte del vestido saliendo de esta cobija blanca que estaba cubriendo todo su cuerpo. Yo en ese momento ya sabía lo que la enfermera me iba a decir.

Lentamente me acerque hacia ella, no sé de donde saque fuerzas, la abrase y lloré. No me importó manchar mis ropas con su sangre o quien estuviera a mi alrededor porque sabía que esa sería la última vez que la abrazaría, la besaría y que sostendría su mano. Esa noche no dormí, pensando en ella a cada minuto. Cuando apenas la vi que era tan fría, cuando la abrasé por primera vez, cuando nos resfriamos los tres en esa playa tantos recuerdos y cosas que hicimos. Yo no la quería ver el día del entierro. No sabía si iba a poder con todo eso que sentía verla en esa caja, saber que era la última vez que la vería. No poder ver su sonrisa otra vez tal vez solo en fotos, en pocas palabras estaba muerto en vida. Al final me armé de valor y la vi aun ya no estando en este mundo. Se veía tan radiante, recuerdo haberle susurrado unas palabras como cuando lo hice por primera vez cuando le dije que la esperaría hasta el final. Esta vez fue diferente, esta vez dije "Adiós mi amor esto solo es temporal estoy seguro que algún día te veré en esta o la próxima vida ahora tú me tendrás que esperar."

Quería que el tiempo se hubiera detenido para poder admirarla por unos minutos más. Mi amiga estaba ahí, toda la ceremonia estuvimos tomados de la mano, no pudimos contener nuestras lágrimas cuando la estaban bajando porque sabíamos que ya no la podríamos volver a ver nunca más. Cuando la ceremonia se acabó mi amiga me abrazo muy fuerte, yo también la abrase y si otra vez nos volvieron a ganar las lágrimas, porque ya éramos los únicos dos que quedaríamos. Me quedé ahí por un par de horas pensando en todo y tratando de buscar una explicación de porqué esto, porque a mí, porque a esta edad. Sentí que Dios no era justo. Así los días pasaron y aunque me doliera tenía que aceptar la realidad y vivir con ello. Un mes después mi mejor amiga, la chica del autobús, regreso con su familia a su país Puerto Rico. Me despedí de ella en el aeropuerto. Le dije que fue un placer haberla conocido y que ella no tenía la culpa de lo que sucedió y que siempre iba a ser mi mejor amiga aún que pasen ochenta años estemos súper viejitos y sin dientes. Después de esto trate de vivir la vida lo mejor posible. conocí personas en el camino, pero obviamente nunca sería igual. Simplemente me dije a mi mismo tratare de hacerlo lo mejor posible y ahí fue donde nació ese dicho que tengo "hay que vivir un día a la vez."

En pocas palabras diría que en la vida no hay que buscar el amor. El amor no se busca simplemente llega sin previo aviso. Es algo que no se puede ver, se siente, y cuando llega no hay nada que lo detenga. No importa tu raza, color de piel, nivel social, religión, altura o tu nacionalidad, cuando esto llega ni tú mismo lo podrás detener. Puede que trates de mentirte a ti mismo, pero el siempre gana al final. ¿Que si pude encontrar el amor otra vez? Claro que sí, aunque tuve que conocer a otras damas en el camino. Lo cual no me arrepiento, pude conocer secretos y experiencias por así decirlo de otras damas para así poder entenderlas mejor y tratar de hacer lo correcto en todo momento y actuar con todo mi nivel intelectual posible. También tengo que entender que no es Kayla, que es alguien diferente. No la puedo tratar igual, es una persona diferente y que no puedo compararla. Quiero conocerla y seguir enamorándome de ella de una forma diferente cada día.

Jairo Barahona

Nicaraguan

Until I Meet You

The Bus Girl, The Cold Girl and The Romantic Boy

This is a small account of my adolescence, which happened a few years ago, the day I met a beautiful lady who changed my life from here to the moon literally speaking, a story of joy, laughter, sadness, and hope.

It was a pretty sunny morning; that day was my first day of school in a different country and with a different language which I still had not mastered yet. My parents enrolled me in this high school which was about thirty minutes away by bus. The Monday was already there. That day I felt a little nervous because it was a new school with people I did not know. I got up early to take the school bus and waited twenty minutes, and honestly, for me, it became eternal. Then the bus arrived to my surprise. It was the last stop for this bus.

I entered the bus and thought there were too many strangers and few places available to sit; but, in the back of the bus, a beautiful smile and a pair of eyes so fixed were watching me. She just smiled I also did, and without thinking that she would be one of my best friends. Also that one day I had to say goodbye to her and without realizing that she would be one of my best friends and that I would even treat her as part of my family. At that moment, I felt very tense; there were so many things to talk about to this lady and none of them occurred to me. But a few minutes, later everything changed. I think we talked and laughed too much, and I even felt that I knew her all my life. Time passed so quickly, and finally we arrived at a very large school with too many people around. At that time, I asked myself, “Now where do I go?” The good thing is that I had met someone who had already attended many times. Yes, the girl from the bus and to my surprise I was going to be with her in seven of my classes.

I got off the bus but we kept talking as we were walking in the hall of this new place for me, but at the same time a very attractive and interesting place. A few steps before entering the classroom was the moment when I saw her. Wow, I was impressed when I saw her. If beauty could be defined with a single word, then I would not have just a single word to use to describe her. It was incredible how much beauty could fit in this scarce five feet of height. Without thinking at that moment, I got closer to her. I felt a small chill running through my body, and she turned and saw me. The truth was, I felt so vulnerable. I felt as if this look could have pierced my soul and see in her all those emotions I felt for her at that moment. I approached her and said, "Do you know what time it is?" I have to admit it is a bad introduction. She only smiled. At that moment I felt that I melted like an ice cream to about ninety-eight degrees of heat in a sunny day just being in front of her.

We talked for a few minutes. She would also be in my first class. I was so impressed, not only for being so beautiful, but for her way of thinking. She also had a fatal sense of humor equal to mine. Apparently we had something in common. The minutes passed and she attracted me more since she was so kind, so beautiful, so fragile, but very strong. Just listening to her voice, she could give hope to anyone who listened to her including me.

The day had passed very fast, and I remember that I took about seven different classes, and I already wanted to wake up on that Tuesday to see her again. So young and so deluded, I thought that I could conquer the whole world, but I wanted to conquer her heart. Finally, Tuesday arrived. That same morning, I remember getting up earlier so that I could have more time to dress and look better in order to call the attention of this beautiful lady who had me crazy with all these emotions to know her better.

As soon as I got off the bus with my friend, I saw her bus arriving. While she was walking off the bus, I saw her coming with this young gentleman. He was hugging her and even kissed her on the forehead. I felt very strange; maybe I was just starting to be jealous even though I had just met her. I was already lying to myself at that moment. Then in the first class, I was talking to my friend, the girl from the bus, that I met in my first day of school – the one who would be with me in good and bad times. I remember we were joking with another friend, at that time I asked her if she knew the young man who was hugging Kayla. She answered that he was Kayla's brother. I felt foolish to have been so immature, but at the same time I felt very good because there was a possibility to express my feelings to this lady.

The week went by and every day my emotions were stronger for this strange short girl with a charming smile and beautiful hair which came at an unexpected but a very good time. If someone asked me a question like what was my favorite characteristic of this lady? I would say that, "I would take everything!" She was like perfection in person. Well those were the emotions that my foolish heart was feeling for her again. Another Friday was gone, but my mind and my heart were happy because I was going to see this beautiful lady on Monday again.

That first weekend seemed eternal; every minute and second passed very slowly, even if that was the first week I had met her. I longed for Monday to come quickly; and with it, the courage and the hope of being able to tell her what my heart was feeling for her. I really do not know where I got the courage to talk about all these emotions I was feeling for her. The moment I saw her, I told her everything I was feeling for her just the way I had practiced the night before. I expressed my feelings with precise details, and she just smiled. She looked directly into my eyes. I could not forget that look, so direct and penetrating, and even after so many years, I remember it as if it were yesterday. After a few seconds, everything changed in that beautiful moment. She said she was not ready for a relationship at that time. I felt very disappointed. I told myself that I had so many illusions and beautiful emotions and for what? Nothing!

I was so stupid to think such things. Very selfishly, I was just thinking about me and not about her. The days went by, and I still could not get her out of my head. I asked myself why that attitude when I saw her and told her what my heart was feeling. Her attitude betrayed her; her face, her eyes and her whole body were telling me the opposite. My head was spinning. I wondered what I did wrong. I knew that I was not the only boy who was in love with her. There were also two other guys who were dreaming for her. Even though these guys were physically better than me, they could not get what I wanted either. One of them was taller and stronger physically, and the other seemed like a telenovela actor because he had such a good sense of humor that it was difficult not to laugh when he was around.

I also had my qualities; I was not the handsomest or tallest, but I was kinder to her. I listened to her. I gave her hope if she had something that she was not understanding. I tried to help her; although in the end, it was me who ended up needing help. I was more romantic with her. I do not know if that was a virtue or a defect in me since I remember how her face blushed when I was dedicating a poem or a song to her. At the end of the day, she was very different with me; I could even say that we had a connection.

One morning, I was talking to my friend about her, but in my mind I still wondered why she rejected me. I had the thought that this was not a rejection. I asked my friend who already knew Kayla, what I had done, and I asked her why Kayla was like this. I declared my feelings and I'm almost sure she wanted to say yes. My friend answered my question, "Two years ago, Kayla met a young man almost like you, very kind and romantic with her. They became engaged and sincerely they seemed very happy, until one day she found him kissing her best friend. Since then she is so cold, cautious, and does not trust people that much anymore, especially guys." This was the part of the story that I did not know about her. She was so beautiful and so kind but sometimes so cold, with so much pain in her heart and unable to express it with words even if she wanted to. When the class ended, I was outside waiting for her, and I felt that I had to tell her something – that she was not alone anymore, that even when everyone walked away I was going to be there for her from now until the end. Honestly, I did not care who was around me, and I felt as if my body acted without thinking. I hugged her so hard; I was feeling in my heart that I did not want to let her go, and that was the place where she belonged. After a brief moment of having her in my arms, I whispered in her ear saying I was going to wait for her, even if I had to wait days, months or even longer than that. I did not want to live this lonely life without her anymore. I wanted this lady by my side from now on. That smile she gave me after holding her in my arms I had never seen before. At that moment, I wanted to steal a kiss from her lips, but I understood that it was not a good moment; I had to be patient and wait.

As those summer days were almost gone, but even that approaching winter cold season could not cool down those emotions I was feeling for her. Those days were passing much faster, and Kayla and I became closer. Also the girl from the bus was always by our side too. We were something like the three musketeers of the high school. We always were at the parks or the beach on the weekends. That Friday we decided that we would go to the beach on Saturday. I said okay, but in my mind there was another concern. The water would be very cold, so how will I look in a bathing suit – they will look incredible, but I believe that be spaghetti with pants. But, for them, I accepted the challenge. Finally, Saturday was there, and I was not mistaken. They looked magnificent, but I was lucky that we had good weather. The sun was shining with all its power until ten in the morning. Then it got very cold, and I did not get along very well with the cold water, so I sat on the sand wrapped in my towel watching them having fun. We were there all day. We enjoyed the entire day. The three of us were walking back home, and Kayla was too tired to walk. I thought she was exhausted from swimming too much. I told her that I would like to take her home on my back. At first, she did not want it, but I think I convinced her to carry her on my back until we arrived. I admit that I was already tired, but made it back home thanks to her.

First, we arrived at her parents' home, but at that moment a hurricane was passing through the state and strong rains and many thunderstorms were normal in Florida. It was lightning, so her parents asked me to spend the night there with them because it was very dangerous to leave because of the storm. It was our luck that day that a hurricane was passing through this state. I was not at all upset to spend all day with them. That night, we also watched a movie. What could be better than that? The movie ended and only the three of us were awake. I would stay on the couch while she and the bus girl slept in her room. When I was saying goodnight to

Kayla, she hugged me. Honestly, I could not resist, and I turned around and kissed her. She did not dislike it this time. I did not have to ask if she wanted to be my girlfriend. She asked me if I wanted to be her boyfriend. I felt like I was dreaming. I did not have any idea if this was going to work out, but I had her in my arms. I felt very lucky, and I had peace in my heart finally.

On Sunday, we spent the day together. This time it was just the two of us. Time went so fast this day. Then another Monday came, but this time we walked together, grabbing each other's hands in the halls of the school. I saw those two young guys, the ones who were interested in her. They looked directly in my eyes. I was not angry, but in my mind I said, "Sorry gentlemen, the difference is that I was born for her, and that nobody would take her away from me while I live in her heart and while she loves me." Every day I felt more alive with her as if I could die and be reborn again with her.

Christmas was approaching. On Saturday, we were planning to go dancing with everyone in the class. The reason for the dance was that it would be the last year that the class would be together, and the following year many would leave this school while others would be in other classes including me.

Every day Kayla smiled more and more sincerely. She made me happy only with a simple expression on her face, and she did not have any idea the things she was doing to my heart. The day before the dance she showed me her dress she had just bought and said, "I hope you like it. I bought it thinking of you." While I kissed her, she just smiled. That day I would be waiting for her, and she would arrive with my best friend, the girl from the bus. I was waiting for about forty minutes and thought she was a little late because she was having problems with her make up. That's what I wanted to think. The minutes went by, and I worried. I called her parents who said they did not have any idea where she was. She never showed up, and the reason was that a drunk driver did not obey a red light; he impacted her car. Unfortunately, Kayla died before reaching the hospital.

About ten minutes later, I received a call from her father, and he told me that they were in the hospital and that they still did not know why. I wanted to think that everything was fine and that it was not serious. I arrived to the hospital and felt crazy. Then a nurse came and took me to this room where they were. First I saw my best friend; she had a very beaten arm and was a little purple with a few small cuts. The good news was that she was going to be ok. Then I was taken to this other room when I saw a part of the dress coming out of this white blanket that was covering her entire body. At that time, I already knew what the nurse was going to tell me.

Slowly I walked closer to her; I did not know where I got that strength, and I cried and did not care about staining my clothes with her blood or who was around me because I knew that it would be the last time I would hug her, kiss her, and hold her hand. That night I did not sleep, and I thought about her every minute. I remembered when I hugged her for the first time and when the three of us had that special day on that beach. There were so many memories about things we did. I did not want to see her the day of the burial. I did not know if I was going to be able to deal with all that pain I was feeling to see her in that box, and that it would the last time I would see her. I would not be able to see her smile again except maybe just in photos. I got dressed; I do not know where I got that courage, and I saw that she was in another place already. She looked so radiant. I remember whispering a few words in her ear as I did for the first time when I told her I would wait until the end. This time was different; this time I said, "Goodbye my love. This is only temporary. I am sure that someday I will see you in this or the next life. Now you will have to wait for me."

I wanted time to stop in that moment to admire her for a few minutes more. My friend was there, and during the whole ceremony we were holding hands. We could not contain our tears when they were coming down the aisle because we knew that we would never see her again. Then when the ceremony was over, my friend hugged me very hard, and I also hugged her and again those tears were coming down because we were the only two that would remain. When the ceremony was over, I stayed there for a couple of hours thinking about everything and trying to seek an explanation of why this, why me, why at this age. I felt that God was not fair. So the days went by and although it was killing me, I had to accept the reality and live with it. One month later, my best friend, the bus girl, returned with her family to her country Puerto Rico. I said goodbye to her at the airport. I said it was a pleasure to have met her and she was not going to be blamed for what happened and she was always going to be my best friend even after eighty years had passed and we were very old and toothless. After this, I tried to live my life the best possible; I met people, but it would never be the same. I just said to myself that I would try to do my best, and that's the reason I always say that you have to live one day at a time.

In a few words, I would say that in this life you do not have to look for love. You do not search for love; it simply arrives without warning. It is something that you cannot see, but you will feel it when it arrives. There is nothing that can stop it, no matter your race, color of your skin, social level, religion, height, or your nationality. When this arrives, you may hide it or you may try to lie to yourself, but love always wins at the end. Did I ever love again? Of course I did. I met other ladies on the way which I do not regret. Now I am more prepared and experienced as well to speak and be patient, to listen to other ladies so that I can understand them better and try to do the right thing at all times and act at an intellectual level. I also have to understand that this lady is not Kayla; she is someone different that I cannot treat her like if she were the love of my past. She is a different person, and I cannot compare her. She is simply beautiful and special, and I want to meet her and continue to fall in love with her in a different way every day.

Jairo Barahona
© 2017
Nicaraguan

Injusticia Social

Hablar de injusticias sociales es hablar de todo un mundo de diversidad de opiniones lo cual nos tomaría todo el libro de explicar. Tomando en cuenta en que existen un sin número de situaciones a las que podríamos llamar de esta manera y entonces esto dejaría de ser una historia de mi vida o un poco más que una opinión. Entiendo que lo más probable es que no muchos estén de acuerdo con mi manera de pensar y sobre todo de actuar, pero esto es lo que a mí me ha tocado sentir y vivir por lo cual no puedo tener otra opinión. Es importante para mi mencionar que el propósito de abordar este tema no es victimizarse si no más bien, analizar una situación que hoy me toca vivir. Pero sobre todo la idea principal es provocar un debate emocional en el interior de quien lo lee. Considero que todos como parte de una sociedad nos podríamos beneficiar si tratamos de entender un poco las situaciones ajenas. Creo que llega una etapa en la vida en la que nos damos cuenta de que nadie es víctima de nadie solo de nuestras propias decisiones. En algunas ocasiones la vida nos pone a prueba en situaciones que jamás hubiéramos esperado como me está pasando a mí. En mi caso la vida no ha sido fácil y por supuesto he tomado malas decisiones que como en todo acto han tenido consecuencias y estoy consciente de que muchas de estas podrían haberse evitado pero la pregunta entonces es ¿Quién elige equivocarse? Vivimos en un mundo en el que al parecer a pesar de estar en el siglo 21 las mujeres estamos obligadas a cumplir con ciertas expectativas sociales que en la mayoría de las ocasiones no satisfacen nuestras propias necesidades. Algunos ejemplos son: Tener que cumplir con obligaciones en el hogar, en la familia, en la escuela, aportar a la economía, además en el trabajo y siempre viviendo en una continua comparación con el sexo opuesto. Sin que suene a feminismo, pero es como si tuviéramos que comprobar nuestra capacidad, nuestra integridad o intelecto. Tal parece que nacimos para satisfacer necesidades ajenas y no las nuestras, pues a una mujer que se atreve a tomar iniciativas a cambiar los roles, ser independiente autosuficiente, salir de la rutina, tomar riesgos y el control de su propia vida no es bien vista. Sobre todo, en algunos países particularmente hablando, lo peor del caso es que las mismas mujeres hagamos parte de este sistema de condena social.

Me llamo Iris y esta es mi historia. Yo a mis 32 años de edad soy madre soltera de tres hijos, el mayor de 11 años, la mediana de 7 años, y el menor de 5 años. Tuve una infancia muy feliz y aunque carezco de muchas cosas materialmente hablando considero que el mejor ejemplo de mis padres ha sido enseñarme que rico no es el que tiene, si no el que sabe compartir y es feliz con lo que tiene.

Cuando tenía 20 años me enamore de un personaje lleno de problemas y que al igual que yo tenía ganas de comerme el mundo. Pero en fin ahí estábamos los dos tratando de construir una historia juntos. Yo al principio de verdad creí que podía ayudarlo a salir de sus problemas de drogadicción y por un tiempo así fue. Aunque la realidad me daba duro en la cara. Yo me aferraba a la idea de ser algo así como su salvación claro que en ese entonces yo no conocía de Dios, pero definitivamente estaba convencida de que ayudarlo era mi misión en esta vida. Como no hay mal que dure cien años esto tuvo un fin y duró 4 años y tuvo como resultado un hijo. hasta que tuve que tomar una decisión que en ese entonces me resultaba muy difícil de asimilar Yo me crecí en un hogar con mamá, papá e hijos todos juntos en las buenas y en las malas. Por supuesto que eso hubiera querido ofrecerle a mi hijo, algo así como una estabilidad emocional familiar.

Después de esto conocí a otro personaje y con la esperanza de poder contar una historia diferente comencé de nuevo. Me casé y tuve dos hijos más, pero la realidad es que el remedio fue peor que la enfermedad. Viví seis años tratando de encajar en un mundo en el que por más que me esforzara no había manera de entrar sola era un mundo de dos y con esto me refiero al término pareja. Mi ex esposo tiene una manera muy diferente de pensar a la mía correcta o incorrecta no lo sé, digamos que tenemos diferentes conceptos de la palabra felicidad. Yo como que no tenía mayor oportunidad de cambiar o modificar eso. Ni siquiera estoy segura de que fuera lo ideal, de verdad que me esforcé por cumplir con mi rol de buena esposa, buena madre, mujer abnegada y entregada a una vida de iglesia trabajo y familia. Los resultados no fueron los mejores y con esto no quiero decir que este estilo de vida sea malo o que no funcione solo que en mi caso digamos que no fue la mejor manera. Y aunque adoro a mis hijos no pude darles lo que ellos se merecen, tener una familia estable. Después de mucho tiempo y de un largo proceso de autovaloración, entendí que hay cosas que se salen de nuestro control o que simplemente no están en nuestras manos pues el amor no se mendiga ni se forzar. Una persona simplemente te ama o no te ama es así de simple.

Después de recoger los pedacitos que quedaban de mí y con la firme decisión de levantarme y tomar el control de mi vida hoy me encuentro con muchos más obstáculos que al principio de esta historia. No solo los económicos si no, también los ideales eclesiales que te condenan más que Dios y que en la mayoría de los casos vienen más de los prejuicios e ignorancia social que de la misma Iglesia. Tal parece que la sociedad me hubiera puesto una etiqueta de fracasada. Tal parece que no tuviera el derecho de buscar mi felicidad y de poder ofrecerles a mis hijos esa estabilidad emocional que tanto anhelo. De llegar algún día a sentirme llena, completa y plena y sinceramente esto es algo que se me hace totalmente injusto porque yo respeto la vida ajena y aunque estoy consciente de mis errores me pregunto, ¿Quién no ha cometido errores? Y, sobre todo, ¿Quién está exento de cometerlos?

Hoy se lo que valgo, sé muy bien lo que quiero y lo que no quiero en la vida y también sé que lo más probable es que como todo ser humano algún día me vuelva a equivocar, pero he aprendido a aceptarme y a perdonarme a mí misma. La vida me ha enseñado que en ocasiones la mejor manera de ganar es precisamente perdiendo, pero sobre todo me di cuenta de que el peor error de mi vida no ha sido casarme, ni conocer a estos hombres, ni tener tres hijos, mi peor error sin duda alguna ha sido poner mi confianza en un mortal porque cualquiera me va a fallar no por malos ni por buenos si no por nuestra propia naturaleza. Hoy vivo con la convicción de que hay que aprender a poner los ojos más hacia arriba en aquel que no te falla, que te cuida, que es capaz de dar su vida por ti como ningún otro ser tiene la capacidad de hacerlo y la diferencia está en su naturaleza divina. Soy fiel creyente de Dios y por lo tanto de la justicia divina y es por eso que a veces me pregunto si no sería mejor que solo le dejáramos la justicia a Dios, ya que Él es el único juez al que le debemos tener amor y temor. Esta solo es una humilde opinión y a todos los que lean esta historia les pido que antes de hablar o juzgar a alguien mejor piensen en que la vida da muchas vueltas. No sabemos cuándo nos va a tocar estar del otro lado y esta es solo una opinión.

¿Que si creo en el amor? Definitivamente si, pero no en esa clase de amor de telenovela. Si no en aquel que viene del alma, el verdadero, el puro, el eterno, el sincero como el de una madre por un hijo incondicional. El que ya casi nadie tiene la capacidad de dar, sé que la vida me tiene preparado algo hermoso. Me gusta pensar de esta manera, me motiva a ser mejor cada día y sobre todo sueno con poderles dar a mis hijos esa estabilidad emocional que tanto necesitamos todos y siento que es lo que ellos merecen. Esa es mi deuda con ellos.

Iris Longinos

Mexicana

Social Injustice

To speak of social injustice is to speak of a whole world of diversity and of opinions which could take the whole book to explain. There are a number of situations that could be called social injustices, but then this would stop being a story of my life or little more than an opinion. I understand that most probably not many agree with my way of thinking and above all of acting, but this is what I have felt and lived so I cannot have another opinion. It is important for me to mention that the purpose of addressing this issue is not to victimize me. Rather, to analyze a situation that today I have to live with. Mostly, the main idea is to provoke an emotional debate inside who reads it. I consider that all people, as part of a society, could benefit if we try to understand a little of the situations of others. I believe that there is a stage in life when we realize that nobody is a victim of anyone but our own decisions. In some occasions, life tests us in situations that we would never have wanted. In my case, life has not been easy; and, of course, I have made bad decisions that have had consequences and I am aware of. Many of these could have been avoided, but the question then is who chooses to make a mistake? We live in a world in which apparently despite the fact that we are in the 21st century, women are forced to comply with certain social expectations that in most cases do not satisfy our own needs. Some examples are: having to fulfill obligations in the home, in the family, in school, and to contribute to the economy in addition to working and always living in a continuous comparison with the opposite sex. It is as if we had to check our capacity, our integrity, or intellect. It seems that we were born to satisfy the needs of others and not ours, for a woman who dares to take initiatives, to change roles, to be independent and self-sufficient, to leave the routine, to take risks and control of her own life is not well seen especially in some countries. Particularly speaking, the worst of this case is that women should be part of this system of social condemnation.

My name is Iris, and this is my story. At 32 years of age, I am a single mother of three children; the oldest is 11, the middle is 7, and the baby is not yet 5. I had a very happy childhood, although I lacked many things materially speaking. I consider that the best example of my parents has been to teach me that a rich person is not the one who has, but the one who knows how to share and is happy with what he has.

When I was 20, I fell in love with a character full of problems. We were both trying to build a story together. I really believed that I could help him with his problems with drug addiction and for a while I did. Although the reality hit me hard in the face, I clung to the idea of being his salvation, but it was clear that at that time I did not know God, but I was definitely convinced that I was helping him. It was my mission in this life to help stop this evil, but it came to an end after a hard 4 years and this marriage resulted in a child. I had to make a decision that at that time I found it very difficult to assimilate. Since I grew up in a home with mom and dad, I wanted to have my children all together in good and bad. Of course, I would have wanted to offer my son emotional stability.

After this, I met another gentleman and was hoping to be able to tell a different story and start again. I married and had two more children, but the reality is that the remedy was worse than the illness. I lived for six years trying to fit into a world and although I worked hard at it, I was to be alone in a world with two children. My ex-husband had a very different way of thinking about what right or wrong is. I do not know, let's say we have different concepts of the word happiness. I did not have the greater opportunity to change or modify that. I am not even sure that it was the ideal truth that would force me to fulfill my role as good wife, good mother, selfless woman and be delivered to a life of church work and family. The results were not the best, and with this I do not want to say that this lifestyle is bad or does not work, only in my case we say that was not the best way. Although I love my children, I could not give them what they deserve and have a stable family. After a long time, I understood that there are things that are out of our control or that are simply not in our hands because love is not mandated or forced. A person simply loves you or does not love you – it is that simple.

After collecting the remaining pieces of myself and with the firm decision to get up and take control of my life, today I find many more obstacles than at the beginning of this story. There are not only economic struggles, but also the ideals that condemn you. In most cases, there are more prejudices and social ignorance and the Church itself seems to have been labeled as a failure. So it seems that I did not have the right to seek my happiness and be able to offer my children that emotional stability that I long for, to someday feel fulfilled. Sincerely, this is something that seems totally unfair because I respect the life of others and although I am aware of my errors, I ask myself, "Who has not made mistakes?"

Today, I know what I'm worth. I know what I want and what I do not want in life, and I also know that most likely, as every human does, that I will continue to make mistakes, but I've learned to accept myself and to forgive myself. Life taught me that sometimes the best way to win is losing. I realized that the worst pain of my life was not to marry, to meet these men, or to have three children, my worst pain without a doubt has been to put my trust in a mortal because anyone is going to fail me because it is human nature. Today I live with the conviction that you have to learn to put your eyes upwards in the one who does not fail you, who cares for you, who is able to give you life. No other being has the ability to do it, and the difference is His divine nature. I am a faithful believer of God and therefore of divine justice, and that is why I sometimes wonder if it would not be better to just leave justice to God since He is the only judge we should have love and fear. This is only a humble opinion and all who read this story, I ask that before talking or judging someone to think that life takes many turns.

Do I believe in love? Definitely, yes, but not in that kind of telenovela love. Love must come from the soul, the true, the pure, the eternal, like the unconditional love a mother has for a son. I know that life has me prepared me for something beautiful. I like to think in this way, and it motivates me to be better every day and above all dream with power to give my children that emotional stability that we need so much we all feel that they deserve. It is my debt to them.

Iris Longinos
© 2017
Mexican

Amor Descubierto

Ella iba caminando sola por la calle
Pensando "Dios, qué complicado es esto del amor"
Se preguntó a sí misma cuál habrá sido el detalle
Que seguro Cupido malinterpretó
El daba como cada noche vueltas en la cama
Sonó de pronto una canción romántica en la radio
Quizá fue la canción quien metió el dedo en la llaga
Y como le faltaba el sueño fui a buscarlo
Los dos estaban caminando en el mismo sentido
Y no hablo de la dirección errante de sus pasos
El la miró, ella contestó con un suspiro
Y el Universo conspiró para abrazarlos
Dos extraños bailando bajo la luna
Se convierten en amantes al compás
De esa extraña melodía, que algunos llaman destino
Y otros prefieren llamar, casualidad
Y él le preguntó al oído
Mi amor, ¿dónde estabas?
Durante todo el tiempo que yo te busqué
Ella le contestó lo siento, es que estuve ocupada
Aunque para serte sincera, ahora no entiendo en qué
La noche se hizo día, pero no se fue la luna
Se quedó a verlos apoyada en el hombro del sol
Alúmbrales con fuerza, brilla todo el día
Y cuando llegue la noche, yo sellaré su pasión

Yuribia Palacios
© 2017
Mexicana

Discovered Love

She was walking alone down the street
Thinking, "God, how complicated love is"
She wondered what details about love that
Cupid's arrow had been misinterpreted.
He returned to her bed every night.
A romantic song on the radio suddenly sounded
Maybe it was this song that
love forced his finger into my open wound
And since my dream of love was missing,
I went to look for it
They were both walking in the same direction
He looked at her, and she answered with a sigh
And the Universe conspired to embrace them
Two strangers dancing under the moon
Become compassionate lovers
Of that strange melody, which some call destiny
And others prefer to call it chance
And he asked in her ear
My love, where were you?
All this time, I have searched for you
She said sorry, I was so busy
To be honest, now, I do not understand why
The night became day, but the moon did not go and hide
It stayed to see the lovers leaning on the shoulder of the sun
Grow with strength, shine all day
And when night comes, I will seal your passion.

Yuribia Palacios
© 2017
Mexican

Las Piramides de Teotihuacan

No se sabe quién construyó las pirámides de Teotihuacán, se presume que eran los antepasados toltecas de los aztecas. No dejaron registros escritos. Las pirámides son muy diferentes de las construidas en la arquitectura egipcia. Las pirámides de origen teotihuacano son tan altas como edificios de viente pisos sobre la meseta central de México, con una grandeza y el misterio que despierta la imaginación. Estos edificios se orientan generalmente al oeste siguiendo el movimiento solar y presentan evidencias de sacrificios humanos. Ya estaban antes de los aztecas, que consideraban a Teotihuacán la ciudad de los dioses.

Las pirámides de Teotihuacán son tres;

La Piramide del Sol

Tenía una altura superior a los setenta y cinco metros, pero hoy solo alcanza los sesenta y cuatro metros. En la punta de la pirámide hay una piedra enérgica como atracción turística. El edificio consta de cinco conglomerados truncados superpuestos y una estructura de tres lados que no alcanza la altura de la primera plataforma. En la pirámide hay ocho kilómetros de túneles realizados por arqueólogos según, el arqueólogo Eduardo Matos Moctezuma. La pirámide del sol se dividió hacia las cuatro direcciones del universo, de acuerdo con a la cosmovisión mesoamericana tiene que ver con el rastro de los centros ceremoniales. La única vía de acceso era la calzada de los muertos y se accedía por la escalera de su fachada que asegura que era un espacio de gran santidad.

Piramide de la Luna

Ambas construcciones están alineadas con las estrellas y el sistema solar desde los puntos de levantamiento precisos en la sierra cercana. Con conocimientos avanzados de matemáticas, geometría y astronomía son un interesante ejemplo de arqueoastronomía. Junto a esta pirámide había una estatua llamada una diosa de la agricultura que los arqueólogos colocan en primitivos tiempos toltecas. La pirámide de la luna tiene una planta rectangular, es de ciento cincuenta metros de largo este-oeste y ciento treinta metros en el norte sur, con una altura actualmente de cuarenta y dos metros en la parte delantera de la pirámide. Un cuerpo sobresaliente, más grande que el de la estructura unida a la parte delantera de la pirámide del sol, parece estar unido y no parece ser una superposición, sino que forma parte de la misma construcción. Esta estructura presenta cuatro cuerpos escalonados con paredes en tablero de talud a ambos lados de este cuerpo superpuesto. Hay dos grandes canales de drenaje delimitados por vigas.

La Piramide de la Serpiente Emplumada

Esta se encuentra en la ciudadela. Es un conjunto arquitectónico situado en el lado oeste de la calzada de los muertos. El conjunto forma un cuadrado cuadrangular grande de aproximadamente cuatrocientos metros por lado y fue construido a lo largo de los años d.c. Está rodeado por trece templos secundarios construidos sobre una plataforma. Detrás del templo de las serpientes emplumadas hay dos complejos habitacionales que podrían ser reservados para la élite teotihuacana. En el centro de la plaza hay un santuario con cuatro escalones que da acceso a la plataforma. La pirámide de la serpiente emplumada se encuentra a cierta distancia de las dos grandes pirámides del sol y de la luna, en el camino de los muertos. Fue descubierto en mil novecientos veinte dos. Con un robot exploraron un estrecho túnel de cien metros de largo que conduce al centro inferior de la pirámide donde hay tres cámaras que se presumen destinadas a enterramientos de personajes muy importantes de la ciudad. La cubierta es totalmente barro para que las personas que son introdujeran aquí no se percibieron para continuar el túnel más allá de la pequeña entrada.

Erick Guzman
© 2017
Mexicano

The Pyramids of Teotihuacan

It is not known who built the pyramids of Teotihuacan, seemingly they were the Toltec ancestors of the Aztecs. They did not leave written records. The pyramids are very different from those built in Egyptian architecture. The pyramids of the original Teotihuacan are as high as buildings of twenty flats on the central plateau of Mexico with a greatness and the mystery that awakens the mind's eye. These buildings are generally facing the west following the solar movement and present evidence of human sacrifices. They were already there before the Aztecs, who considered Teotihuacan the city of the gods.

The Pyramid of the Sun

The Pyramid of the Sun had a superior height equivalent to seventy-five meters, but today it only reaches sixty-four meters. At the pinnacle of the pyramid, there is a magical stone that serves as a tourist attraction. The building consists of five overlapping shortened conglomerates and a three-sided structure that does not reach the height of the first platform. There is a sacred place inside the pyramid and it has eight kilometers of tunnels made by the original builders, according to archaeologist Eduardo Matos Montezuma. The pyramid of the sun is divided into the four directions of the universe in accordance to the Mesoamerican cosmology. The only access road was the Causeway of the Dead and was accessed by the staircase on its façade, which assures that it was a space of great sanctity.

Pyramid of the Moon

The pyramid of the moon is aligned with the stars and the solar system from the precise survey points in the nearby mountains. With advanced knowledge of mathematics, geometry and astronomy these are an interesting example of archeoastronomy. Next to this pyramid there was a statue of a goddess of agriculture that archaeologists place in primitive Toltec times. The pyramid of the moon has a rectangular shape, is one hundred and fifty meters long east-west and one hundred thirty meters in the south-north with a current height of forty-two meters at the front of the pyramid. An expanded body, larger than that of the structure attached to the front of the pyramid of the sun, appears to be attached and does not appear to be an overlap but forms part of the same construction. This structure has four stairways with walls that slope. On both sides of these are two large drainage channels.

The Pyramid of the Feathered Serpent

This pyramid is located in the citadel. It is an architectural structure located on the west side of the Causeway of the Dead. The structure forms a large quadrangular square of approximately 400 meters per side and was built in the early A.D. It is surrounded by thirteen secondary temples built on a platform. Behind the temple of the feathered serpents are two housing complexes that could be reserved for the Teotihuacan elite. In the center of the square there is a sanctuary with four steps that gives access to the platform. The Pyramid of the Feathered Serpent is located some distance from the two great pyramids of the Sun and the Moon, on the Causeway of the Dead. It was discovered in nineteen hundred twenty-two. A narrow tunnel was discovered with robots that is a hundred meters long that leads to the lower center of the pyramid where there are three chambers that are presumed destined for burial sites of very important personages of the city. There is a false cover made of mud so that intruders could not continue down the tunnel beyond the small entrance.

Erick Guzman
© 2017
Mexican

Sueño de Niño

Hola solo quiero contarle una parte de la vida de un niño que pueda servirte de motivación para no rendirte ante los retos que te pone la vida. Tus propósitos en el futuro son motivación a seguir preparándote para lograr tus metas importantes. No importa cuánto puedas obtener de tus esfuerzos de estudio o de trabajo. Lo que importa es sentirte orgulloso con lo que lograste. Acuérdate que tanto de tu tiempo te tomó para lograr ese resultado. Este niño es parte de muchas inspiraciones no importa cuántos problemas tengas en la vida. Los problemas son parte de tu preparación para ser mejor. Siempre gánale a la vida que la vida te está ganando, esta es parte de su vida que te voy a contar.

Los padres eran unos humildes campesinos de un pequeño pueblo llamado San Miguel Amatitlán, que al enterarse que iban a tener un hijo decidieron mudarse a una ciudad para darle un mejor futuro a su hijo. Llegaron con unos familiares que les dieron techo mientras encontraban trabajo y donde vivir. Pasaron un par de meses hasta que encontraron trabajo y donde vivir. Una familia les ofreció trabajo en su casa a los dos. La madre se encargaría de mantener limpio su hogar y el padre se encargaría de mantener su jardín. Ellos vivían en una zona de familias con un nivel económico mucho mejor. Las personas de esa zona no los querían por ser de pueblo. A la mama no le importó, pero el padre no se sentía tan contento con el poco trabajo que tenía porque no les alcanzaba para las necesidades que tenían.

Así que se decidió a buscar más trabajo y lo encontró en construcción. Su pago era mejor pero el trabajo era muy cansado. Así que empezó a consumir alcohol para no sentir el cansancio. Llegaba a casa todo tomado y siempre tenía problemas con su mujer, hasta que llegó el día que iba nacer su hijo y se dio cuenta que su esposa necesitaba más de él. Decidió buscar trabajo más cerca de casa para cuidar de su hijo y su esposa.

Los años pasaron, el niño creció, y empezó a ir a la escuela. Conoció a muchos amiguitos y para él, era mucha diversión. Con el tiempo, se dio cuenta que en su casa algo no estaba bien. En una ocasión el niño se dio cuenta de los maltratos que hacía su padre a su madre. Desde ese momento empezaron a cambiar las cosas para él. La diversión ya no era como antes. El solo pensaba cómo ayudar a su madre a trabajar.

Cuando regresaba de la escuela le ayudaba a su madre a limpiar los hogares, aunque no era suficiente. Mientras que él le ayudaba con los trabajos, siempre se preguntaba porque su padre la maltrataba. El decidió de enfrentar a su padre y decirle que ya basta los maltratos hacia su mama, le pregunto qué es lo que lo hacía enfurecer si su mamá también trabajaba.

El niño siempre le pedía a su madre que no lo llevara a la escuela, él quería trabajar con ella para ya no depender de su padre. Su madre con lágrimas en los ojos le dijo nunca hagas lo mismo que tu padre, siempre respeta a los demás para que te respeten, estudia, edúcate, y aprende todo lo que puedes. Algún día tu tendrás una familia y un hogar, siempre piensa en tu futuro como lo vas a formar.

Pasaron los años hasta que un día tuvieron que regresar al pueblo de donde eran sus padres. El niño le pregunto porque tenían que mudarse de su hogar. Su madre le explicó que su abuela estaba enferma y que tenía que cuidarla. Al niño le empezaba a regresar la felicidad porque al fin iba a conocer a más familiares.

Cuando llegaron a ese lugar, el niño vio una casa muy grande y vieja y le preguntó a su madre a donde estaba su familia porque él estaba ansioso de conocerlos. Pero su madre dijo que eso tomaría tiempo y que lo primero era cuidar de su abuela. Después de una semana, sus padres se habían establecidos en su nuevo hogar. Trajeron a su abuela, el niño feliz por conocerla platicó mucho rato con ella. Le pregunto cuánto tiempo se quedaría con él. Su abuela le dijo que hasta que recuperara y pudiera caminar. El niño contento le dijo que él la cuidaría hasta que se sentiría mejor. El padre se tuvo que marchar a trabajar muy lejos y solo regresaba unos días de descanso.

Su madre lo llevó a la escuela para que regresara a sus estudios. El niño se sentía más tranquilo porque su padre no estaba en casa y empezó a estudiar. Pasaron los años, el niño empezó a ser un adolescente. Un día fue a la escuela y cuando regreso a casa le dieron una mala noticia que su abuela estaba en el hospital. El joven preguntó que tenía porque él había cuidado de ella. La madre le explicó que la abuela ya era muy grande de edad. El joven fue a verla al hospital y le preguntó si se sentía bien. Su abuela le contestó que solo era la edad y que ya era muy vieja y su cuerpo ya no aguantaba como cuando era joven. Estuvo con ella unos días en el hospital, pero su madre le pidió de regresar a sus estudios y de cuidar de la casa mientras ella cuidaba a su abuela.

El joven regresó a su casa y pasaron los días. Su madre luego regreso a casa y le dijo que su abuela estaba mejor para que no se preocuparía por ella. Después de unos días el joven no sabía más de ella y le preguntó a su madre que como seguía su abuela. La madre le tuvo que contar la verdad y le dijo que no había dinero para pagar los gastos del hospital, que los medicamentos eran muy caros. El joven desesperado le dijo a su madre que él se iba a trabajar, pero su madre le dijo que no, que ellos verían como pagar los gastos del hospital.

Pasaron los días hasta que recibió la mala noticia que su abuela había fallecido. El joven, triste y con mucho coraje porque él no pudo hacer nada para que su abuelita, decidió en ese momento de cambiar su forma de pensar. Se preguntó cómo le iba hacer para seguir estudiando si no había ni para comer. Su padre ya no regresaba a casa, se la pasaba gastándose el dinero en alcohol. Su madre tuvo que quedarse a cargo del hogar y el joven decidió de trabajar para ayudar a su madre. Se dedicaron a cuidar el ganado y cosechar sus propios alimentos. El joven se sentía contento porque ya le ayudaba a su madre. Su madre quería que él seguiría estudiando, pero él estaba preocupado por si algún día ella se enfermara quería que tuvieran dinero para curar a su madre.

Un día, cuando el joven cumplió 14 años, decidió hablar con su madre porque quería irse al extranjero para poder trabajar más. Así decidió emigrarse a otro país donde sus amistades le decían que en el aquel país había mucho trabajo y que les iba bien y que tenían lo que ellos querían. Su madre no pudo contener sus lágrimas y le dijo que si es lo que él quería ella no podría hacer nada. Ella sabía que este joven ya no pensaba como un adolescente que él ya tenía pensamientos de un adulto.

Pensaba que si se ponía a trabajar a su corta edad tendría su propio hogar, ayudaría a su madre para que ella no se preocupara más y que su padre entendería que ya no necesitaría de él. Ahora él trabaja ganando buen dinero y ya tiene su propia familia y él empieza a formar su propio hogar. Aunque él ha dejado a sus padres ellos están muy orgullosos de lo que él ha logrado. Pero más importante, un niño que soñaba de ser amado, ya es padre de dos hermosos niños y da bienestar y amor a su esposa. Y… este niño está estudiando clases de universidad y está logrando mucho en este nuevo mundo llamado mi sueño.

Etbaruc G. Vazquez
© 2017
Mexicano

A Child's Dream

Hello, I just want to tell you a part of the life of a child that can serve as a motivation to not surrender to the challenges that life puts you through. Goals are the motivation which prepares you to achieve important milestones. No matter how much you can obtain, your efforts of study or work is what matters; to feel proud of what you achieved is the best feeling of them all. I agree that it will take a lot of your time to achieve that result. This child is part of many inspirations that forced this story to be told. No matter how many problems you have in life, problems are going to be in your way as you prepare to be a better person. Always aim to win. Life is winning; this is part of a life achievement that I would like to talk to you about.

The parents were humble peasants of a small town called San Miguel Amatitlan. Upon learning that they were going to have a son decided to move to a city to provide a better future for him. They arrived at their relative's place, and they were given a ceiling over their heads while they searched for work. They spent a couple of months there until they found work. A family offered them both work in their home, and they would be in charge of keeping this family's home clean. The father would be in charge of maintaining the family's garden. They lived in a community of families who had a much better economic level. The people of that area did not want them to be in town. The mother did not care, but the father was not so happy with the little work that he had because it did not meet all of their needs.

As the breadwinner of the family, the father went to look for more jobs and found work in construction. Their paychecks were better, but he was very tired so he started to consume alcohol. He was always in trouble with his wife until the day when his son was born, and he realized that his wife needed more support and resources. The father looked for work closer to home to take care of his son and his wife.

The years passed and they sent the little boy to school. He had many friends and enjoyed life. However, eventually, he realized that in his house something was not right. On one occasion the child became aware of the abuse that his father was doing to his mother. From that moment, the boy began to change. Things he had done for fun were not like it was before. He focused on how he could help his mother at work.

When he returned home from school, he would help his mother clean homes. Although it was not sufficient, he helped as best as he could. While he worked, he always wondered why his father mistreated his mother. She worked every day, and one afternoon, he confronted his father and told him to quit mistreating his mother. He asked him what makes him so angry about her.

The boy would always ask his mother not to take him to school. He wanted to work with his mother so she would no longer depend on her husband. With tears in her eyes, his mother told him never do the same as his father. Always respect others and they will respect you. Study and learn as much as possible. Someday, you will have a family and a home. Always think about your future as you are going to make it your life's purpose.

The years passed until one day they had to return to the town where the parents had once lived. The boy asked his parents why they had to move back to their old home. His mother explained that his grandmother was sick and that she had to take care of her. The child returned back to his old happy self because, at last, he would know more relatives and could go to school again.

When they arrived at the place, the boy saw a very large, old house. His mother told her son it was going to take time to get settled in, and the first thing they were going to do was take care of his grandmother. After being there one week, his parents became established in their old home. They introduced him to his grandmother. He spoke to her for a very long time. He asked how long she would stay with him. The grandmother told him it would be until she recovered and could start walking again. The happy child told her that he would take care of her and make her feel better. The father had to go to work very far away, and he only returned home just for a few days to rest.

His mother took him to school to start studying again. The child felt more calm because his father was not at home and he could study without the stress. He spent the years as an adolescent trying to be a man. One day, he went to school, and when he returned home, they gave him the bad news that his grandmother was in the hospital. The young man asked what was wrong with her as he had taken care of his grandmother. His mother explained that it was her age, that she was already very old. The young man went to see her in the hospital and asked her how she felt. His grandmother replied that she was very old and her body could not take much more. He was with her a few days in the hospital, but his mother asked him to go back to his studies and take care of the house while she took care of his grandmother.

The young man returned home and days passed. His mother later returned and told her son that his grandmother was better so he would not worry about her. The days went by and he did not hear any more about his grandmother. He asked his mother how his grandmother was doing. She told him the truth, that she did not have the money to pay for the hospital and the drugs were very expensive. The desperate young man told his mother that he was going to find a job so he could pay for his grandmother's medicine. But his mother told him not to worry about it, they would manage.

Days passed and he received news that his grandmother had died. The young man became very sad and very angry because he could not help his grandmother. He decided at that moment to change his way of thinking. He asked himself why he should keep studying when he had not food. His father no longer returned home; he spent his money on alcohol. His mother had to stay and carry on the tasks at home. They took care of the livestock, harvested their own food, and the young man was happy because he could help his mother at home. He would work a lot so that one day if she got sick they would have money to take care of his mother.

One day, when the young boy had turned 14 years-old, the young man decided to talk with his mother because he wanted to go abroad to work more hours and get better pay. He wanted to immigrate to another country where his friends told him he could find a lot of work and that he could do well. His mother told him if he wanted to have a good future she would have to let him go. His mother could not contain her tears and said that if it is what he wanted she could do nothing to keep him there. She knew that this young man was no longer a boy. He already had thoughts of an adult.

When he came to America, he started to work at his young age. He realized he could have his own home. He would help his mother so that she would not have to worry anymore, and his father would understand that he was not needed anymore. Now, he works making good money, and he already has his own family and is starting a new home for his family. Both of his parents are proud of what he has achieved. But most importantly, a child who had dream of being loved is now a father who is providing the love and comfort to two beautiful children and a wife. And… that child is now attending college classes and is going places in this brave new world called my dream.

Etbaruc G. Vazquez
© 2017
Mexican

Thai To English

ประเพณีและวัฒนธรรมในประเทศไทย

คนไทยมีปีใหม่เหมือนประเทศอื่น ๆ มากที่สุดและเรียกว่าสงกรานต์
มักจะตกระหว่างวันที่ 13-15 เมษายนของทุกปี เรามีความสุขมากที่ได้ร่วมเล่นน้ำกัน
เราไปที่วัดเพื่อชดใช้การละเมิดของเราและอธิษฐานต่อพระพุทธเจ้า
วันที่ 15 เมษายนผู้อาวุโสที่นับถือเทน้ำบนมือเราและขอพรจากพระพุทธเจ้า
ชาวต่างชาติเดินทางมาเที่ยวไทยในเทศกาลสงกรานต์เป็นจำนวนมากในช่วงนี้
ในอดีตคนไทยอายุต่ำกว่า 20 ปีต้องเข้าพิธีบวช
ชายหนุ่มต้องศึกษาพระภิกษุสงฆ์และหลักคำสอนของคนไทยเชื่อว่าการอุปสมบทของลูก
ชายจะนำพ่อแม่ไปยังเกาะสวรรค์เพื่อเป็นการทดแทนพระคุณของผู้ปกครอง

Kanokwan Brown
© 2017
Thailand

Tradition and Culture in Thailand

Thai people have New Year's celebration like most other countries, and it is called Songkran. It usually falls between the days of 13 - 15 of April every year. We are very happy to play in the water together. We go to the temple to make amends for our transgressions and pray to Buddha. On April 15, the revered elders pour water on our hands and ask for blessings from Buddha. Foreigners visit Thailand a lot in Songkran during this time. We also believe in years assigned to animals. These animals are symbolic with specific characteristics. In the past, Thai men under the age of 20 were required to attend the ordination ceremony. Young boys were required to study Monkhood and its doctrine. Thais believe that the ordination of a son will bring parents to the island of heaven as a substitute for parental grace.

Kanokwan Brown

Thailand

Vietnamese To English

CUỘC SỐNG MỚI - ĐẤT NƯỚC MỚI

Sáng thức giấc lại chuẩn bị đi làm.
Về đến nhà khi trời đã tối.
Sống hối hả theo dòng đời bận rộn.
Cuộc sống Mỹ thật không như mơ ước.
Bao khó khăn mà tôi thật thấy khó.
Cố gắng lên Tôi thường nhũ với mình.
Một ngày trôi qua tôi lại thêm một lỗi.
Khi trong mơ tôi nghĩ Mỹ là thiên đường.
Nước phát triển mà mọi người muốn tới.
Bắt đầu lại mặc dù giờ đã muộn.
Đi học thôi bao cái hay đang vẫy gọi.
Đừng lãng phí thời gian ngồi than thở.
Càng khó khăn mình càng thấy mình giỏi hơn.
Rất nhiều thứ mà Tôi cần phải học.
Học lái xe rồi lại học ngôn ngữ.
Và bây giờ Tôi thấy thích nước Mỹ hơn.
Thời tiết tốt và nền giáo dục tốt.
Họ sẵn sàng giúp khi tôi cần giúp đỡ.
Và bây giờ Tôi chỉ cần kiên nhẫn.
Vượt khó khăn cho một tương lai tươi sáng.

Hanh To

Vietnamese

NEW LIFE - NEW COUNTRY

Getting up early and preparing to work.
Arriving home late when it is dark.
My busy life is moving in a constant flow.
The American life is not a dream.
There are a lot of difficulties that I realize
They are very hard.
I try my best.
I usually talk to myself.
mistakes are made every day.
In my dream, I think of America as heaven.
A developed country which many people now call home.
Starting my new life; although it is late now.
Going to school and good things are waiting.
Don't waste the time sitting and complaining.
It is more difficult now that I have grown up.
There are many things I need to learn.
Studying to drive a car and learning English.
I feel that I love America even more now.
Good weather, good education, and good people.
I need to be patient for now, and I shall
overcome the difficulties
and look forward to a bright future of hope.

Hanh To
© 2017
Vietnamese

Cuộc sống ở Mỹ

4 namtrước là 1 cô bé 8 tuổi
bước chăn qua đất nước xa nhà
lúc mới qua tôi còn bơ ngỡ
lúc đến trường tôi không biết một ai
ngồi trong lớp nhưng không biết làm gì cả
sáng đi học đêm về nằm khóc
đối với tôi kinh khủng biết chừng nào
nhưng tôi nghĩ vì cuộc đời có nhiều thử thách
vì như thế tôi có thêm động lực
phải trước qua thử thách của cuộc đời
càng làm tôi yêu cược đời này hơn
va như thế tôi dến trường mõi ngày
tìm cánh thực hiện ước mơ của tôi
nhưng đơi khi không nghỉ tôi còn đến trường được
bởi cuộc sống ở đây tôi phải phải học nhiều thứ
lo đi làm lo nhiều thứ
tôi cảm thấy thời gian của tôi rất hối hả
nhưng lúc trước tôi không ra điều đó
và hôm nay vẫn còn giang nan lắm
nhưng ngày mai nhất định sẽ tươi sáng hơn
và tôi sóng những đóa hoa đẹp nhất
để tỏa ngát hương thơm cho cuộc đời

Lanh To

Vietnamese

Life in America

Four years ago I was an eighteen-year-old girl
Stepping into a country far from home.
At first I was surprised.
At school I did not know anyone.
I sat in class but did not know what to do.
I went to school in the morning crying,
"How terrible to me."
I think life has many challenges.
I have more motivation now.
I must face the challenge of life.
I love this life very much.
I go to school every single day
To find the truth of my dreams.
When I am stressed out, I go to school.
While living here, I have to learn many things.
I am worried about many things.
I feel that time is moving very fast.
Time was slow in my country.
Today still very difficult,
But tomorrow will definitely be brighter.
I have the most beautiful flowers
To radiate the fragrance of life.

Lanh To
© 2017
Vietnamese

From the Editors And Staff

Flight of the Condor

I had hiked in as far as I planned to go this day. I was deep in the Torres del Paine National Park, on the tip of South America in Chile. The hike was spectacular. The topography was vast, rolling hills with tall grasslands where herds of guanacos, a smaller version of the llama, graze next to large lakes of varying hues of blues and greens. Massive rock peaks jut straight up from the lakes which makes this park very popular with rock and mountain climbers. Scenic views are abundant. I had walked to a point where a glacier met a lake and a small foot path lead down to the shore. The ice had a blue color to it when viewed from a distance, but up close it looked almost milky white with streaks of brown and black all over making it look dirty. My traveling companions and I entered an ice cave, a place where the glacier was melting because of its contact to the warmer earth. From the inside, looking up through the ice, the color was a deep blue. As we marveled over the colors and took photos, we heard rumblings from the glacier and decided it was time to get out. Shortly, a large piece of ice calved, broke off from the main glacier, into the lake. A baby iceberg had formed.

During the late 1970's, the park had very rustic cabins that were available to hikers. These "refugios" were free to the hikers but contained not much more than a roof over your head, a table with a couple of chairs and several bunk beds made with hard planks. At least we could get out of the cold wind. We carried backpacks with all our food and cooking facilities as well as our sleeping bags. Since we had been traveling in South America for several months, we did not have access to freeze-dried foods and had to supply ourselves from the local markets in Puerto Natales, a town 115 kilometers away. We carried supplies such as cabbages and onions, pasta and rice, and a few cans of tuna fish. We had left the clothes that we were not wearing in a box at a hotel to make room for the food and to lighten the load.

Late that afternoon, while we were cooking our dinner, we felt a disturbance in the air outside the cabin. We ran out and looked up into the sky. We saw something that looked like a small airplane coming down the valley towards us. For a moment, I flashed on the old World War 2 movies where people would watch the bi-planes fly towards them and then they would get mowed down with gunfire. Well, we didn't dive for cover but kept watching. Soon we could tell that it was a large bird, a very large bird. The bird was the Andean Condor, almost extinct, but still found in this park. The bird's wing span was over 10 feet from tip to tip, and it flew directly over us about 10 to 15 feet above our heads. The updraft created by the movement of the wings was phenomenal. As the bird flew directly over us, it tilted its little head and looked directly at us. In that moment I was so glad that I was too large to be its dinner.

We were extremely lucky to witness this flight of this condor. We talked to many other hikers and climbers during the rest of our trip and asked them had they seen any condors. Condors nest in the very peaks of the mountains and climbers know to avoid them. Some could see them riding the wind thermals high above, but none had seen a condor so close up. We knew our experience was unique and quite mystical.

Kay L. Wolf
© 2017
American
(Editor and Translator)

The Seventh Gift

Kicking the frozen ground and watching the ice spray made me feel better. The harsh winter wind stung my cheeks warmed with tears as I pulled my red hat down over my pigtails. Last night's snow hugged the black trees in Chatham, Pennsylvania. I did not want to go back inside and face my mom.

"No, Dee, we can't afford a pony this year; your father says that ponies are very expensive to feed in the winter. A no means no, and I'm sorry," Mom said. As she poured the potatoes into the boiling water, steam rose from the pot making her strawberry blonde hair curl at the edges of her face. "You will like what we got you dear," she said softly.

"I know," I said. "I'll get the rest of the groceries in," and ran out the back door. I did not want to make her feel bad. I knew we could not afford a pony, not with six children to feed. My dad drove a produce truck, and my mom sewed for people and made our clothes.

I sat on the frozen log and watched the frozen water trickle under the ice covered creek that ran through our yard. It was two days until Christmas and the sky was turning a dark grey. I thought. I do love the snow, especially at Christmas. I looked at my blank Christmas list. It was hopeless; all I could think about was a pony. I let the empty list drop out of my hand onto the frozen creek. I fed the outside animals on our small farm and took the rest of the groceries inside. The warmth of the house felt good on my fingers and cheeks.

Mom smiled at me. "Are you hungry? Dinner will be ready soon," she said.

I nodded and smiled as I went to wash up and let the warm water run over my hands to thaw them. My stomach growled. The smell of hot fresh biscuits in the oven and a stew on the stove made me hungrier. Mom always had a knack for making everything taste good.

After dinner, we all helped clean up the kitchen, and Mom and I made some cookie dough and put it in the refrigerator to cool so we could cut out Christmas cookies the next morning. Then I sat on my dad's lap and watched the news with him.

"A snow storm is moving in Dee, we'll be sledding by Christmas," Dad said.

I nodded. "Yes, that will be fun," I said. I watched my dad in the evening light, his black hair and blue eyes made him look young. I knew he and mom loved us.

The following day was Christmas Eve; the house was full of delicious smells of roast turkey and of freshly baked pies and cookies. I could not help but laugh at the younger kids. They were so excited about what they were getting for Christmas. My older sister Pattie and I spent the day entertaining our four younger siblings and taking turns wrapping gifts.

"You're being stubborn Dee," Pattie said. "You should forget about some old pony. We only get seven gifts and you did not put anything on your list. You may not get anything!"

My heart sank. "I do not want to talk about it," I said. "I have decided to babysit to earn money next summer for my own pony."

Pattie sighed and gave me a hug. "You are so stubborn Dee; you can't afford a pony either," she said.

Finally, it was time to open our one Christmas gift on Christmas Eve. We each received a new pair of pajamas. Mine was a blue nightgown with a ruffle at the bottom.

Dad said, "Dee, you look like a blue sky on a frosty morning."

I gave both of my parents a kiss. Each one of my brothers and sister got a new pair of pajamas in their favorite color. Wow, I thought. How did my parents keep up with the wants and needs of six children?

Christmas morning sunrise peeked over the snowy fields. The sounds of my brothers' and sisters' laughter mingled with the fresh aroma of Christmas breakfast cooking drifted into my room.

Dad hollered from the foot of the stairs. "Dee you're missing everything!"

Reluctantly, I hopped out of my bunk bed that I shared with my little sister, went downstairs, and sat on the bottom step. The cool hardwood floor covered in wrapping paper was cold on my bare feet. Mom handed me five gifts to open: a new sweater, pants, a diary, a new pack of socks, and boots. Then my dad scooped me up in his arms and carried me outside. There on the front porch, stood a silver colored pony with a white mane. He wore a brown saddle and bridle. I hugged my dad's neck as he sat me in the saddle.

"I'm going to call him Silver," I whispered. I buried my hands and feet into his warm coat.

"The farmer who gave him to us said he couldn't use him anymore; he'll spend the rest of his days with you Dee. He can stay in one of the old stalls at the edge of the property." Sliver "snorted" and his breath stood still in the cold air. Dad and I laughed.

Later after giving rides to my brothers and sisters, I walked Silver to his new home. I spotted my empty Christmas list sticking out of the snow. I picked it up and put it in my pocket. I brushed Silver and talked softly to him as he ate. Then I turned over a bucket and wrote a note to my dad.

Thanks Dad, Love Dee.

Karen D. Martin
© 2017
American
(Support Staff)

Vocabulary Lesson

It was just a normal evening of being at home with my husband after a stressful day of teaching tenth grade English at Wildwood High School. I was already in my pajamas even though I rarely went to sleep before *The Tonight Show with Jay Leno.* The phone rang around 9:00.

"Amy, can you come over here real quick? Some folks are here that you need to see." It was my dad. I assumed it was a cousin or a friend paying a late, spontaneous visit. I put on some pants and a t-shirt and found my flip-flops. It was not what I had in mind, but I was curious, so I drove the three miles to my parents' brick house in a quiet neighborhood.

Sitting at Mama's kitchen table were three people I didn't know. A man and woman with a young girl smiled at me but didn't say anything. Daddy tried to explain, "See, Amy, these here people don't know any English. So, I wanted you to come here to talk for me." I was so confused.

"Daddy! I don't know Spanish! I had classes in high school nearly ten years ago. I only know a few words!" Unfortunately, I also hadn't had anyone to practice Spanish with. My co-workers and students who were bilingual spoke in English at the school unless they were talking only to each other.

I was really caught off guard. My mom, standing at the sink washing a few dishes, filled me in, "You, see, your daddy was out at the Waffle House drinking coffee and noticed them having some car trouble in the parking lot. He figured they needed some help because the tire shop is closed for the night. He didn't want them to be stuck at the Waffle House, so he brought them home." I could picture this scene. We lived in a small town in Central Florida, but two major interstates connected out at the truck stop. My daddy was a brakeman for the railroad and also farmed watermelons. After a long day of either riding the rails or riding a tractor in a watermelon field, Daddy would get restless sometimes and go sit at the never-closing Waffle House and maybe strike up a conversation with a traveler or one of the waitresses. There was nothing available after five for a traveling family having transportation problems. My dad's idea of speaking Spanish was yelling English slowly, so I don't even know what he said or did that convinced them to leave their car parked and get in his pickup truck.

I was bewildered that he would pick up strangers and bring them home to my mother and my 16-year-old brother, Kevin. But, they certainly seemed harmless. I could understand how he wanted to help them, as they sat smiling and nodding at the table. I didn't know where to start, "Coffee?" I asked them.

I got nods of yes, and "Si, Si!" So, I gave directions, "Mama, can you put on a pot of coffee for them?" So far, so good. No Español necessary to offer coffee. I put Mama's sugar bowl and some creamer on the table along with two coffee mugs. I smiled and pointed to the refrigerator while holding a glass toward the girl. She stood up and walked the few steps to see what was being offered. I pointed out a gallon of tea, a bottle of Gatorade, and a can of Coke and gave her a questioning look. She put her finger on the Coke. I held it up to her mother and asked, "Ok?" since most moms I knew would not allow a sugary, caffeinated beverage at night. The mom smiled, so I put ice in the glass, opened the can, and poured.

I held up a loaf of bread and shrugged my shoulders, hoping they would figure out that I was offering food. I got even bigger smiles and gestures that they were hungry. I put the bread, peanut butter, and Mama's homemade strawberry jam on the table. I rummaged in the pantry and pulled out some chips. I gave them butter knives for spreading, plates, and napkins and let them do their own sandwich fixing.

"Mama, what do you want for sleeping arrangements?" I asked.

"Well… there's a double bed in Cory's old room…." she thought aloud. My other brother had moved out a couple of years ago. Mama then went to put fresh sheets on that bed and make a pallet on the floor for their daughter. Kevin and Daddy just sat and looked on with amused expressions about this exciting night of such exotic strangers in the house.

While they were eating, I wanted to communicate to figure things out a little and make them comfortable. "Where are you from, dónde?" I asked in my ridiculous version of Spanish. But, it was good enough because they said, "Miami." Miami was about five hours south of Wildwood. So, I assumed that is where they were headed… or maybe where they were coming from. Then, the man said, "To Tehas." Hmmm… oh, Texas! So, they were driving to Texas from Miami. That is a two or three-day trip at best. The lady offered, "Ecuador" which I figured to mean their home country.

My dad yelled at them, "I HAVE A FRIEND WHO IS A MECHANIC. WE WILL GET HIM TO LOOK AT YOUR CAR IN THE MORNING." Their faces were blank. I pointed to my dad and said, "Papa's amigo es… un… automobile… repara." I had just added an o to an English word and hoped. "Ah… Ok… good, good," the man said. I thought, well he might not actually know what I was trying to say, but he seemed to be relieved. I added, "In manana" for a bit of clarification.

Then, I awkwardly announced, "Yo trabajo en escuela." Why did I say that? I just told them that "I work in school", so what? I guess I was just searching for any words that I could share. What else could I say to them? We just smiled at each other. It was too early to expect them to go to bed.

I went to Mama's linen closet and pulled out some clean towels and washrags. Maybe they would want a shower. I held it out to them hoping they wouldn't think I was offering a souvenir. The mother nodded her head and said some things to her daughter. The dad said something more serious sounding to the girl before she stood from the table. They accepted the towels, so I led them to the bathroom and gave them a fresh bar of soap. The mom began preparing a bath for her daughter. The dad went out on the porch to smoke.

I searched for some coloring sheets and crayons and a few toys that my mom still had around from when we were little. I told Daddy to offer the remote because they would know how to find Spanish television. At this point, my job was over. I couldn't do anything more for them, and everyone would settle into bed soon enough. The little girl came out of the bathroom with wet hair and clean pajamas from her bag. I said, "¡Buenas noches!" and waved to them. They returned with, "¡buenas noches!" and "gracias, gracias." I couldn't remember how to say, "You are welcome," so I just smiled and waved again.

Mama and Daddy thanked me and told me good night as I gathered my purse and keys.

That little girl is now an adult, possibly with children of her own. For several years after that unexpected visit, my parents received a Christmas card with written ¡Feliz Navidad! inside. They were postmarked from various towns in Texas. Daddy would ask me what those words said and be so proud that I knew some Spanish. He wasn't even aware of the only Spanish Christmas song that played repetitively on our radio station each December. But, he did know how to recognize when people needed help. Even more importantly, he was generous enough to offer assistance and to give whatever he had to share. That night, he shared more than food and a bed. He offered hospitality and companionship to people even though he could not verbally communicate with them. Vocabulary isn't necessary in order to be kind.

Amy Russ
© 2017
American
Editor

Strands of Many Colors

Her hands were arthritic and uncooperative as she tried to thread her needle. She could barely see the fine hole as she jiggled the thread through the eye. After her third attempt and some saliva on the thread, she finally pulled the elusive strand slowly through the eye. I was just five-years-old when my grandmother made this "strands of colors" for me. I remember vividly as she would patiently gather her fine strips of cloth, thread, safety pins, and scissors. She would lay out each piece, thoughtfully building a unique design to create a story of my lineage – but not just any lineage, a lineage of an unnamed Civil War hero.

Nana had spoken about each piece of cloth and the wealth of history behind each piece as it was sewn into her complex pattern. However, one drably gray strand of cloth stood out amongst the rest which laid in her lap. All of the other pieces were bright and colorful, but this one piece was tattered and looked as if it had been ripped from its original garment. I could not imagine why Nana would want to put this piece into this magnificent piece of work. I remember this conversation with my grandmother as if it was yesterday.

I remembered asking my nana, "Nana, are you going to put that ugly strand into the quilt?" I asked. My grandmother just smiled and said with a faint whisper, "Yes, little one. This is the most important strand of cloth of all."

Nana called to me and put me in her lap. She began to tell me the story about this holey, frazzled, piece of cloth. She took it and showed me a large hole with burnt singes all around it. "Do you know why this hole is important within this piece of cloth?" asked my grandmother. "This cloth was part of a soldier's uniform – but he was not just any soldier. This piece of cloth belonged to the uniform of your great-great-grandfather who fought in the Civil War." I glanced into my nana's eyes trying to understand the concept of war but not fully understanding what she was trying to tell me.

My grandmother explained to me that my grandfather's daddy had fought in a war in Tennessee where brothers fought against each other. She said family members would even kill each other. My daddy had shown me a gun once and told me never to touch it. He said it could really hurt me and sometimes guns would kill people. So, when my grandmother began speaking about the hole, I was naturally curious.

Nana said that my great-great-grandfather had served in the war as a Methodist minister. He didn't believe in war. But because he was from the South, and was recruited by the Army, he had to leave his family behind and join the rest of the men in the community to march toward Georgia. She told me great-great grandfather's name was John Bell Hood, and he led a battle against another man called Sherman. But most importantly, this battle took place at a little church called New Hope Baptist Church located at a place called Pickets Mill.

Nana had always had an old Bible resting on the mantle of the fireplace, but we were never permitted to touch it. It wasn't until I was much older that I realized this Bible had been pierced all the way through with a foreign object. But to continue with my story, Nana said there were only a few men left in grandfather's troop to fight because all of the others had been injured, captured, or killed. They were in this church surrounded with twenty of Sherman's troops waiting to charge in and kill them. My grandfather and his men were running low on ammunition, and it looked as if they would soon die as well.

My grandfather had been against this war from the very beginning, and he had always carried his Bible in his black overcoat for when his men were in need of prayer or needed to be prayed over as they were dying in the fields. Grandfather, not wanting to die before saying a prayer with his men, got down on his knees and asked God to help them. Suddenly, one of grandfather's men had noticed, hidden behind the pulpit, a wooden crate with a skull and crossbones on the side of it. John Bell Hood's prayer had been heard from the heavens because within this box were fifty sticks of dynamite.

Outside the church, Sherman's men were getting closer and closer, and the ammo was running out quickly inside the church. Grandfather devised a plan to save his men by using this dynamite and taking out Sherman and his troops in the process. Within the church was a bootlegger's door that had been discovered near the dynamite crate and concealed underneath the pulpit. The door led to an underground tunnel and out into the woods. Grandfather instructed all of his men, with the exception of his sergeant, to escape through the tunnel and wait for them in the forest.

Sherman and his men were now shooting into the windows of the church, while the soldiers called out for them to surrender. Sherman's men were yelling out profanities, and they were growing more and more anxious to overrun the church. One of Sherman's lieutenants noticed that it had grown quiet in the church. Obtaining permission from Sherman, the men decided to charge the church, thinking that most of the men were too weak or dead to fight back.

Charging the church and taking out the front door, the men entered with rifles and muskets firing. Smoke and sulfur filled the room; but, when the smoke settled, they looked around and discovered that no-one was in the building. The bodies of the dead rested on the pews but great-great-grandfather and the living were nowhere to be seen. One of the Union soldiers had gone to sit down on one of the church pews and decided to pray. As he bowed his head, he noticed a spark scoot past his boot on the floor. It was too late. The whole church exploded. All of the men inside that church died instantly, with the exception of General Sherman and his drummer.

"But Nana, how did my grandfather get that hole in this piece of cloth?" I asked.

"Well, it was like this. Your grandfather had stayed behind to light the last fuse on a bundle of dynamite at the bootlegger's door, so they couldn't follow him through the tunnel. As grandfather John [Bell Hood] lit the wick, a Union soldier came down the ladder toward where your grandfather was hiding. Your grandfather began to run when he heard the soldier entering the tunnel. The Union soldier hollered at grandfather to stop and surrender, and when your grandfather turned around to see this man, the Union soldier shot him, leaving your grandfather for dead. All of the dynamite exploded right after that… killing all of the soldiers inside the church and the one man at the entrance of the tunnel. The thing is, your grandfather did not die in that tunnel. The Bible he carried in his jacket pocket took most of the force of the bullet and it just barely entered his skin. Your grandfather realized that he wasn't dead and sneaked back into the woods with his men, thus stopping the Union army from delivering ammunition to their troops on the battle lines. The actions of your great-great grandfather saved 1,400 men in that war that day."

Today, that quilt hangs in a glass frame centered on my wall in the living room. Many strands, squares, and strips are in that quilt, each with its own unique story. Just wait until I tell you about the one piece of cloth with black and white stripes and a partially faded number on it. It is a doozy… But that will have to be told another day.

Dr. Patricia H. Graham
© 2017
American
(Compiler, Editor, Translator)

www.ingramcontent.com/pod-product-compliance
Lightning Source LLC
Chambersburg PA
CBHW061738050726
47598CB00002B/524

* 9 7 8 1 6 0 8 6 2 7 0 4 2 *